COACH!

ANDREW NEITLICH

FIRST EDITION

Center for Executive Coaching,
Publishing Division, Sarasota FL

Published by Center for Executive Coaching,
Publishing Division, Sarasota FL

Every effort has been made to obtain permissions for material quoted throughout the book. If any required acknowledgments have been omitted, or any rights overlooked, it is unintentional. Please notify the publisher of any omission, and it will be rectified in future editions.

ISBN 978-0-9976287-0-8

Library of Congress Control Number: 2016908383

Cover design by William Reynolds
Interior design and formatting by William Reynolds

Printed in the United States

COACH!

CONTENTS

Part Three - More Coaching Conversations

Part Four - Coaching Situations
Individual Effectiveness

Part Five - Coaching Situations
Strong Relationships

Part Six - Coaching Situations
Supporting Organizational Initiatives

Introduction

The Difference That Coaching Makes

Coaching has had a profound impact on my life. The best managers in my career were generous enough to be coaches as well as managers. They used coaching as a tool to help me reach new levels of success. By sitting down with me and asking probing questions, they helped me come up with my own observations, insights, and new ways of approaching problems. They gave me the capacity and confidence to advance my career and also to lead others, but these managers didn't just coach. They also mentored me, taught me, and, when required, directed me. I remember most the coaching conversations because they left me with lessons that are now part of who I am.

In contrast, my least effective managers came from the command-and-control school of management. They expected me to do what they said. Why? Just because. One of my worst managers once said, "Andrew, your job here is not to think but to execute." I'm not sure why he recruited MBAs from the top business schools if that was his philosophy. Regardless, I left that company - as did many of my talented colleagues - within only a year of joining.

Now that I run a coaching and leadership advisory practice, I enjoy the privilege of working with amazing clients. All of them recognize that even with the success they have achieved they can still get better. Some face challenges that hold back their careers and organizations. Others want a sounding board to test their ideas in a safe, confidential forum. Still others hire a coach to keep improving their game - the same way athletes have a coach to help them keep getting faster, stronger, and gain an edge. This work has proven to me that coaching can achieve extraordinary results.

At the same time, for the past fifteen years, I have run the Center for Executive Coaching, which trains and certifies professionals to become coaches. Approximately a thousand people have graduated from one of our training programs. When they arrive for training, they are already successful whether as leaders, business owners, or experts in a particular discipline. Almost all of them share that their most rewarding career experiences have involved both being coached and coaching and developing others to higher levels of performance. Some also note that they decided to become a coach after experiencing the benefits of coaching whether from a practicing coach or from a manager who took an interest in their development.

Some people reading this book are full-time coaches whether internal or external. Others are leaders and managers seeking to develop coaching as a skill. Some coach in a for-profit setting, while others coach in a nonprofit or government setting. To avoid confusion throughout this book, here is clarification of three terms.

First, when I use the word "coach," I am referring to anyone stepping into the role of coach. It doesn't matter whether you are a full-time coach or a manager who uses coaching as a skill to develop and engage your people.

Second, when talking about coaching, this book is focused on coaching people in organizations to be more effective in their roles. Sometimes this kind of coaching is called leadership coaching, executive coaching, management coaching, high-potential coaching, career coaching, development plan coaching, team coaching, or corporate coaching. Coaching may be defined by the sector, as in corporate coaching, nonprofit coaching, government coaching, and educational coaching. Coaches seem to love to make up new terms, and I am sure I have left out some possibilities. To keep things simple, I am going to call all of these things coaching. The key emphasis is on coaching professionals to higher levels of performance.

Third, to avoid having to write "the person being coached" every time we discuss the person you are coaching, I use the word "client" or the phrase "coaching client." Your so-called client might be an employee who has come to you for coaching, or it could be a colleague in an organization where you serve as an internal coach. Perhaps it is a paying client if you run a coaching practice. Even if the client is not paying you, I am still referring to the person being coached as a client.

Again, the emphasis should be on practicing coaching and getting results, not on splitting hairs about terminology. Coaching is fun and productive. Splitting hairs regarding terminology isn't.

Coaching is emerging from its infancy as a profession. Professional coaching associations can be found, and a common language for coaching and some clear core competencies define effective coaching. Research has documented the efficacy and returns of coaching, although common sense would indicate that receiving the support that effective coaching provides would have an impact.

Even as coaching evolves, a great many organizations, leaders, and managers haven't yet embraced it as a tool to develop and retain top talent. My intent with this book is to give you a practical guide without the jargon that unfortunately clouds many coach training programs today to get great results by adding coaching to your capabilities.

The rewards of coaching are fantastic. What leader wouldn't want the ability to help other people advance their careers, develop new skills, and move their organizations forward?

Enjoy!

Part One

FOUNDATIONS

What Coaching Is And Isn't

Coaching has many definitions, and many coaching associations have their own definitions of coaching along with sets of core competencies. This book defines coaching with a primary focus on coaching leaders, managers, and up-and-coming talent in organizations:

Coaching is an efficient, high-impact process of dialogue that helps highly performing people improve results in ways that are sustained over time.

Unlike traditional consulting assignments, coaching is efficient because it does not require invasive processes, large outside teams, or lengthy reports and analyses to get results.

It is a high-impact process because coaching typically gets results in short meetings, which can often last only a few minutes and are rarely longer than an hour. During this time, the coach and the individual being coached can generate important insights, gain clarity, focus, and make decisions to improve performance

Coaching is a dialogue. The coach and the person being coached are working together to make things happen. When you are coaching, you might speak 25 percent of the time, while the other person speaks 75 percent. Even if you are an expert in your field and know all the answers, you hold back to let the person being coached express concerns, challenges, and feelings. The dialogue allows the other person to determine their own answers and action steps, allowing the individual to not only solve immediate issues but also develop the capacity to keep improving.

Third, coaching works with high-performing people. It is not therapy meant to fix a person. As a coach in an organization, you work with people who are already highly functioning and successful. Like any of us, these professionals need support from time to time to perform better. Some might have serious blind spots, such as a leader who comes across as too abrasive, but coaching assumes that people have tremendous talent and potential.

Finally, your goal as a coach is to improve results in ways that are sustainable over time. The point of coaching is to achieve some sort of valuable outcome, usually related to improved performance, higher profits, career success, organizational effectiveness, or career and personal satisfaction. If you aren't helping people get results through coaching, you aren't coaching well. At the same time, coaching is about helping people improve their own capabilities and effectiveness so that the results and performance improvements last. To use the time-worn and famous quote, you are teaching people to fish, not feeding them for a day.

You can incorporate coaching into almost any role.

If you are a manager, coaching becomes a crucial skill to develop your people, improve performance, and gain leverage on your time.

Likewise, if you have a training role, coaching provides a way to sustain results. It makes common sense that following up after a training event reinforces learning and results. For instance, the coach can help the other person deal with specific challenges that might be preventing the training from having its full impact.

Similarly, if you are a management consultant, you probably already provide coaching as part of what you do. Coaching is the part of the engagement where you work one-on-one with clients to encourage them to make difficult decisions, step out of their comfort zone, stop destructive behavior, embrace change, and shift performance. For me, a long-time consultant, coaching is the fun part. Coaching lets you stop doing the analyses (and most of the time the client already knows the answer anyway), stop revising the PowerPoint presentation, and sit down face-to-face with the client to help them improve results. It's the part of the engagement where the client turns to you as their objective, trusted advisor—as a colleague and confidant.

It is also important to be clear about what coaching is NOT.

As noted before, coaching is not therapy. You are not fixing anybody. You are not delving into traumatic pasts. Good coaching certainly gets underneath the surface to look at perceptions, but the emphasis is on helping a healthy individual overcome challenges and be more effective. If you do work with someone who might need therapy, refer that person to a licensed professional.

Second, coaching is also not the same thing as management. Coaching is one tool that a manager can use, but it is not the only tool. Sometimes a manager needs to direct, tell, mentor, and/or teach. Coaching is a powerful skill but not the only thing that a good manager does.

Third, coaching is not consulting. Your primary focus is not to analyze and make recommendations. When appropriate and when you have permission, you can add a lot of value by sharing your own observations and insights, but coaching is more about having the other person develop their own insights and then take new actions to improve results.

Put another way, your job as a coach is not to be a "crystal ball" that magically provides an answer. As a coach, you will intervene and provide advice when appropriate. Successful coaches engage in dialogue with their clients and then customize a tool or solution that works for their unique solution. Sometimes there is no easy answer, and your value will be to support your clients in making decisions with incomplete information.

Fourth, coaching is not training or teaching, which focus on sharing knowledge and best practices and also helping people develop and hone skills. Learning usually occurs in a classroom setting, and the trainer or teacher leads the session. A coach might include teaching and training in the session, and good teachers and trainers coach, but the primary activities in each discipline are different.

Fifth, coaching isn't mentoring. Mentors are typically seasoned professionals within an organization who show less senior and experienced people the ropes. Mentors are great at pointing out how things work in an organization along with some of the hidden keys to getting things done and being successful. They also make introductions and sometimes pull strings. Again, there is overlap with coaching. The best mentors typically coach, and many coaches have years of experience to share with the people they are coaching.

Finally, coaching is not progressive discipline. Many organizations confuse the two, which sometimes causes coaching to be seen negatively. Progressive discipline, or probation, is a process of working with employees who are not performing, with the intent of documenting their poor performance and terminating their employment if they don't improve. In the past, this process was conflated with coaching. The word coaching was—and still is in some organizations—a euphemism for the last resort before firing someone. Today, coaching is seen as a standard leadership development tool. It is an investment in the talent the organization wants to develop and retain. Coaching should be separated from anything related to progressive discipline or probation.

Confused? Join the club. There is a lot of overlap among these different disciplines, and not everyone agrees on where the boundaries stop and start. My advice is that you not spend too much time obsessing about definitions. You can go online and see all sorts of self-appointed coaching police telling people what is and isn't coaching. Instead, do two things:

First, practice and keep getting better at coaching as you go through this book. You will learn firsthand about coaching and what it can do.

Second, and most importantly, if you focus more on having impact and helping the people you coach get results, everything will work out great.

Clearing Up Some Differences with Sports Coaching

Coach n 1: (sports) someone in charge of training an athlete or a team 2: a person who gives private instruction (as in singing or acting) 3: a railcar where passengers ride 4: a carriage pulled by four horses with one driver 5: a vehicle carrying many passengers; used for public transport.

-Source: WordNet ® 2.0 via www.dictionary.com

The above, dictionary definition of a coach is interesting because the first reference is to sports coaching. Many coaches who coach leaders, executives, managers, and up-and-coming talent don't like comparing what they do to what sports coaches do. When people think of the word coach, however, they usually think of sports coaches. Plus, it is hard to argue with the dictionary when it associates coaching with sports coaches.

Let's compare traditional sports coaches with the types of coaches described in this book - coaches who work with leaders, managers, and up-and-coming talent. Such coaches tend to meet with our clients in an office setting, where we sit down in a meeting room and coach. Coaching for us largely entails asking many questions so that clients can determine what to do on their own. We provide advice and observations but try to do so only when clients have exhausted their options.

During the heat of an athletic contest, when most people get to observe sports coaches, we don't see much of this kind of coaching. Sports coaches are much more active, drawing up diagrams, putting players in and taking them out of the game, calling time-outs, yelling at the referees, giving quick remarks to motivate the players, and shouting as they walk up and down the sidelines. They also have a role in recruiting players, cutting players, and setting salaries.

In other words, sports coaches are primarily managers. They manage games, and depending on their level of authority and relationship with the general manager, they also help manage their team.

Behind the scenes, though, top sports coaches sit down with the athletes on their teams and do indeed coach them. They watch tapes to learn what went well and what the athlete and team can do better. They ask questions and engage in a dialogue to understand the athletes' perspective about their performance. They make resources available for the player to train and improve, and then they try to connect with the players so that they take accountability for improving their own performance. Some coaches have more of a command-and-control approach, tending to tell players what they need to do. Others are better at engaging the players in a dialogue to understand what drives them, what makes them tick, and how they can take responsibility for improving their own performance.

Coaches who work with executives, managers, and up-and-coming talent can learn from sports coaches, especially the ones who know how to engage their players. Asking a never-ending circle of open-ended questions, as some coaching associations require, is not always the best way for a coach to get results. In real-world coaching, sometimes the coach needs to intervene a bit more proactively as a sports coach might. An effective coach sometimes makes observations, gives tough advice and feedback and, when needed, even gives a firm kick in the pants.

If you manage and coach a team of employees, the lines get even more fluid. Like a sports coach, you wear many hats, depending on your job description and span of control.

Moving away from the sports coach metaphor for a moment, notice the third, fourth, and fifth definitions of the word coach. These definitions focus on the coach as a vehicle. Personally, I like this more traditional definition best. Think of yourself as a railcar or carriage that gets people from where they are to where they want to be. You are a vehicle that moves individuals, teams, and sometimes the people in an entire organization from their current point A to a better point B.

Why People Who Work with Coaches Are Better

This week I started a coaching engagement with a young leader who hired me to become what he calls "a leader of leaders" within his Fortune 500 company. When we explored his aspirations during our first meeting, it occurred to me for the umpteenth time that leaders who hire coaches are just better: more open, more fun to work with, more willing to learn, more willing to stretch for outstanding achievements, more willing to take responsibility, more concerned about the development of their people, more willing to laugh at themselves, and more positive.

In this case, the up-and-coming executive shared some wonderful goals for himself, his employees, and his area of responsibility. He had the self-awareness and wisdom to know that employing a coach could help him have insights about the most effective and efficient ways to get where he wants.

To his credit, he is paying for the coaching with his own money because his company doesn't support external coaching. He had hired a coach a couple of years ago and got so much value out of the experience that he is doing it again, and I am privileged to be the coach that he chose.

Leaders like my new client come across differently from their colleagues who are not so coachable. They are like professional athletes who are committed to being the best and who hire a team to help them stay in shape and keep improving. They have that sense of drive, an internal fire, and the wisdom that an outside perspective is crucial for their ongoing improvement. These qualities are infectious and make them more attractive to others. One could argue that these attributes alone - even without a coach - will lead to success, and yet these individuals are still willing to hire a coach to get even further, faster.

Clearly, I'm not talking about people upon whom coaching is forced. That's the old way of coaching - in companies where coaching and progressive discipline are still synonyms or in companies that hire a coach as a last resort primarily as a way to document for legal purposes that they tried something before firing the employee. When coaching is forced on someone, he or she rarely wants to be coached.

Unfortunately, despite various studies proving that coaching provides important career and organizational benefits, many leaders still do not want a coach. They will sometimes point to members of their team and say to the coach, "Go fix them. They are the ones who need help." However, they don't see the benefits of coaching for themselves, at least until something really negative happens in their careers, and by then it is often too late.

There is a different feel to leaders who are closed to coaching, at least from my admittedly biased perspective. They come across as a bit more shutdown, unwilling to explore new possibilities, and perhaps even stagnant. They don't like asking for or listening to advice and feedback from others and tend to get defensive when constructive advice is offered. Sometimes they seem more concerned with other priorities than getting results, such as looking good, being the smartest person in the room, dominating others, or winning some sort of popularity contest. They often have some sort of behavioral blind spot, for instance, getting angry too quickly, avoiding appropriate conflict, or letting their egos get in the way of getting results and building positive business relationships. Like the villagers in the story about the emperor who had no clothes, no one in the organization dares to give them a hint that they have opportunities to improve, and they don't believe the messenger, usually from Human Resources, when he or she comes with bad news. Eventually, they get pushed out, never reach the next level, or burn out. This situation is a tragedy, because with a little bit of coaching and a mind-set of being coachable, they could find new ways to get results and thrive.

One other category of a leader is relevant to this discussion: the leader who has a coach but never does anything despite the coach's best efforts. These leaders like the status of having a coach but aren't really interested in making positive change. A coach is more like a status symbol to them, a way of saying, "Hey, I'm on the leading edge of the coaching trend. I have a coach with amazing credentials and a best-selling book. I'm getting enlightened as we speak. Now leave me alone." That's not the type of leader I am talking about in this chapter either.

Shown below are five attributes that I especially appreciate in leaders that hire a coach with the sincere intent of getting better, advancing their careers, and improving their organizations. You might have a different list or some tweaks to this one. If so, please let me know.

They are committed to continuous learning and improvement. By definition, coaching clients want to get better; otherwise, they wouldn't have hired a coach in the first place. It is refreshing to work with people who seek ongoing improvement compared with those who want to preserve the status quo, complete a list of tasks every day, and hope nothing changes.

Their high aspirations are exciting and often lead to great things. Leaders who seek out coaching usually have ambitious aspirations. They want to see great things happen, and people gravitate toward those with vision and a sense of purpose. At the same time, they hold themselves accountable for achieving their aspirations and goals, including ongoing gains in performance.

They see possibility in themselves and others. It is more enjoyable to be around people who see the potential for greatness all around them than to be around people who are cynical, apathetic, and perceive the people on their team to be subpar. This sense of possibility makes them more attractive to others and gets people aligned toward a common purpose.

They are willing to be vulnerable in ways that allow them to leapfrog over other leaders. The best leaders have some degree of vulnerability about them. It is not easy to learn the truth about how we actually come across to others compared with how we hope we come across to others. It is not easy to take responsibility for improving a strained professional relationship, to see one's own role in the situation, and proactively make amends. It is not easy to hear feedback from our colleagues and then resolve to improve. It is not easy to allow give and take when pushing an idea forward rather than win at all costs. This kind of vulnerability, however, ultimately leads to improved results, relationships, and success. Leaders who are vulnerable also tend to attract more followers—especially top talent—than those who are pushy, obnoxious, and unwilling to lighten up. By having just enough vulnerability, they are able to learn, grow, and get better.

They are more flexible in how they get results, which gives them more options. One benefit of coaching is that it often helps leaders develop new approaches to handle different situations. Many leaders are like the proverbial broken clock stuck on one time: They stick to a single style that is right once or twice each day and wrong the rest of the time. Leaders who are coachable understand the need to be flexible and have a range of styles and approaches for different people and situations. This allows them to lead more naturally and authentically instead of relying on long-standing patterns that make them rigid.

In essence, leaders who have coaches have a different quality about them and are better. I am so grateful to be in the coaching profession because it allows me to work with the best of the best.

Why Organizations With a Culture of Coaching Are Better

If an individual who works willingly with a coach is better, it makes sense that an entire organization filled with people who are receptive to coaching is better too.

Coaching is not a panacea that can solve all of a company's problems. It is also not the only tool available to develop talent in an organization, but it can make a company better, and it deserves a place as one of the most important tools to improve performance. Visit the International Coach Federation website (coachfederation.org) for the latest research about the benefits and results of coaching. According to most studies, coaching returns $4 to $8 for every dollar invested. The benefits of coaching to organizations include the following:

- improved loyalty by the people being coached
- improved relationships up, down, and across the organization
- improved teamwork
- improved productivity

Once you know how coaching works, it makes common sense that coaching brings the above benefits. Coaching enables people to discuss issues beyond analytic content. The people being coached start to focus on how well they relate to others, they learn about working with different styles, and they collaborate more willingly and effectively. They have open, honest conversations that are deeper than the usual progress reviews and often come up with innovative ideas that can have a major impact on their teams and organizations. People being coached are encouraged to seek out and listen to advice from others rather than getting defensive. As part of the coaching process, they also commit to making specific improvements in their behavior and attitude. They are better able to balance ego, results, and relationships in their work so that they make things happen while nurturing their relationships with colleagues. Would that type of process make a difference in your organization?

While a culture of coaching might seem touchy-feely, it isn't. Effective coaching includes metrics to track, measure, and achieve results. It also includes conversations to hold people accountable, get underneath the issues, and get things back on track.

Coaching works well in all sectors, including organizations with highly specialized, technical, scientific, or clinical professionals, because it helps people develop the softer skills that they might not have learned during their years of education. They can then take ideas and use influence to get buy-in and execute more quickly and effectively. From biotech firms to Wall Street financial companies, law firms, and emerging technology companies, coaching can broaden the skills and tools that employees need to get results.

It also makes sense that employees in organizations that support coaching are more motivated and loyal because they recognize that leadership is willing to invest in their development beyond the usual, generic, off-the-shelf training programs. High-potential talent quickly gets bored by the generic leadership training programs on the market, which is why it is estimated that billions of dollars are wasted every year on leadership training that doesn't even make a dent on performance. In contrast, organizations that encourage leaders and managers to coach and be coached are able to create personalized approaches to developing talent.

The substance of coaching is quite powerful, too, and helps people work better on teams, lead more effectively, and communicate with more impact. The content you will read in this book offers approaches to help people get better in these areas.

Where would you rather work: in an organization that bakes coaching into its very fabric or in an organization with a traditional command-and-control approach to getting things done? Where do you think the freshest talent coming out of the best schools wants to work? In this respect, organizations with a culture of coaching are also better because they are more likely to attract top talent.

Imagine a company in which every single leader and manager knows how to coach their team members to improved performance. Imagine that each leader and manager sits down with each team member and develops a personalized coaching plan to develop that team member and then follows through with that plan. Furthermore, imagine that as people receive coaching they are more receptive to listen to advice, to examine how well they relate to others, and to commit to making improvements. They have open conversations about their progress and keep working to get even better. What would be possible in an organization in which every employee is committed to this process?

It doesn't have to take much time to make this happen. Coaching can happen during normal one-on-one update meetings; it can happen in short bursts while doing rounds in the workplace; it can happen as part of implementing key strategic initiatives, and it can happen during both formal and informal performance reviews. If leadership is committed, they can create a culture of coaching.

Examples of Situations That Are Opportunities for Coaching

Coaching solves specific problems. The problem can be vague, as in "I just want a sounding board to bounce ideas around" or "I want to become a better leader." Usually, however, the client has a specific issue to address. Common challenges include the following:

- I am juggling too many priorities and feel overwhelmed.
- My career has reached a plateau, and I want it to advance.
- I have a conflict that is hurting my ability to get things done.
- Our team is not working well together.
- We need a strategy.
- We have a strategy, but it isn't being implemented.
- People are resisting change.
- I need a succession plan.
- I received feedback that I need to correct a certain behavior because it is hurting performance.
- My employees are not engaged.
- I need to change the culture.
- I need more leadership presence.
- I need to influence people with more impact.
- I need to manage my time better.

- I can't determine how to get the organization to embrace r
- We need a stronger board of directors.
- I need to develop more leaders.
- Our organization has reached a point where we need to put into place systems and processes before we can improve.
- I need to prepare for my exit from this company.
- I want us to be better at collaborating.
- We don't execute well.
- I need a stronger personal brand.
- I am not getting along well with my manager.
- I need a strong network of business relationships.
- I love technology but not working with people.
- I want more accountability from my people.
- We need to change how we do things, and the organization is not moving quickly enough.
- I am spending too much time at the office and need to delegate more.
- I am too much of a perfectionist.
- We need to improve quality.
- We need to improve our revenues and profits.

Many more examples could be provided, but these are some areas where coaching is valuable. Coaching solves problems. When you hear someone complain about a pressing issue, you have an opportunity to coach them if they are willing.

This leads to the first rule of coaching . . .

The First Rule of Coaching

The first rule of coaching is that you can only coach people who want to be coached. It is a simple rule, and yet aspiring coaches break the rule all the time. Coaching only becomes possible when two conditions are met:

First, someone faces a challenge that is significant enough for that person to want to be coached. This condition is not easy to meet. For most people, deciding to get coaching is like deciding to go to the doctor. Nobody wants to go to a doctor because doing so makes us feel vulnerable and exposed. We only go when we feel enough pain. Being coached also makes us feel vulnerable and exposed at least until we build trust with the coach. For this reason, people rarely want coaching unless they have a big enough problem and enough pain to want support.

Second, permission must be granted. Either the coach asks permission to coach the other person, or the other person asks for coaching. Anyone with a spouse or significant other knows that coaching without permission is not coaching; it is nagging.

With this in mind, people don't naturally seek out coaching. Effective people in organizations typically believe they can figure things out on their own. They don't want help. They don't want others involved in their business, and they definitely don't want to be exposed. Often, they don't even think they have a problem!

Accordingly, the way to find people who want coaching is not by pitching coaching to people who probably don't want to be coached. Nobody wakes up in the morning and says, "I'm a horrible leader. I better go get some coaching today."

The way to find people who want coaching is by finding people who have problems that they recognize as problems and asking them if they would be open to coaching. Alternatively, someone with a problem might come to you and ask for coaching.

Complications arise when we make assumptions that people who should get coaching actually want coaching. For instance, I trained a coach who thought she had secured her first coaching prospect. She explained, "I know lots of middle managers at the company, and they tell me that the senior leadership team is doing all sorts of things that are demoralizing. They are abusive. They are arrogant. They don't listen. They don't seem to care, but I can't figure out how to get the senior leaders to hire me as a coach so they can change these behaviors."

In fact, senior leaders in this company don't necessarily want coaching. The middle managers would like to see them get coached, but there is no indication that the leaders themselves see a problem or want to change. The coach could work with the middle managers if they have the budget to learn to adapt to or cope with the senior team to be more effective, but as long as they are the only ones who acknowledge a problem the senior leaders are not going to ask for coaching.

Coaching someone who is not coachable is like trying to coach a vampire to stop biting. It's not going to happen. The vampire is made to bite! Maybe the villagers living near the vampire's castle want the vampire to change through coaching, but the vampire doesn't. The vampire might be open to coaching about how to recruit more vampires or how best to use his minions assuming he has a challenge in those areas. Likewise, the villagers might be open to coaching about how to protect each other from being bitten, but until the vampire realizes that he doesn't want to bite people anymore or someone can convince the vampire that biting is not in his interests, there will be no coaching on that topic.

Please heed this first and fundamental rule of coaching. Nobody wants unsolicited coaching.

How Coachable are You?

A corollary to the first rule of coaching is that coaches should set the highest standard of being coachable. This sounds obvious, yet many people get into coaching more as an escape or as a way to show they are above other people. They hide behind their coaching certification, use jargon to show that they stand apart, or go to self-proclaimed transformational workshops with a bit of an air of superiority. Some want to be seen as gurus who are above it all. Some are rigid, defensive, and don't listen well. This is not good for the profession. If you are going to use coaching skills effectively, a good starting point is to develop your ability to be coachable.

Someone who is truly coachable is willing to learn from anyone and anything. Instead of getting defensive and taking things personally, the coachable professional uses both achievements and setbacks as opportunities to learn. That person is constantly trying to improve and committed to personal and professional growth.

When people offer advice or constructive feedback to someone who is coachable, that person listens to it, directs it to understand and learn more, thanks the other person, and makes amends for past behavior if they have not been as effective as they could have been. Then they consider the feedback and advice and decide how best to use it in the future. If the advice is valid and helpful, they use it to get even better.

The coachable individual also appreciates that different people have different ways of communicating, thinking, making decisions, relating to groups, getting things done, and leading. They even have different energy levels. Someone who is coachable works hard to develop a flexible style to work effectively with different people in different situations.

Perhaps the best way to develop coachability is by having a coach. At the same time, get into the habit of asking others for their advice about strengths you can build on and ways you can be even better. Listen to the advice. Feel any natural resistance you have to receiving it. Then take it in and process it with the intent of learning and improving based on how helpful the advice is for you. Here are some questions to answer to confirm that you are coachable:

- How open are you when people give you advice or feedback?

- How well do you respond to advice or feedback that points out a mistake you made or something you could have done better?

- How focused are you on constant learning and ongoing professional and personal development?

- How aware are you about styles that differ from you own? How well do you adapt to other people's styles so that you can build rapport with them and develop effective solutions?

What else can you do to be more coachable?

The Fundamental Coaching Conversation

The fundamental coaching conversation is called active inquiry, which combines powerful questions, active listening, and dialogue with the client so that the client receives insights to overcome challenges. Four steps are involved in active inquiry:

First, agree on the intent of the coaching session. Without a clear intent, the session will tend to meander or ramble along without achieving much of importance. Ask the client, "What would be a great outcome to achieve in our coaching session?" Take your time to be sure the client's intent is specific, measurable, and something both of you can achieve in the time you have.

Second, let the client know you are going to be doing active inquiry. For example, "To achieve this goal, I'm going to ask you some open-ended questions. The intent of these questions is to better understand the challenge you are facing and hopefully have you come up with some ideas to overcome it. Is that okay?" Setting up active inquiry in this way is helpful for a couple of reasons. Most importantly, if you don't, and then start asking the client open-ended questions, that person might get confused and think, "Why are you asking me all of these questions?" By setting up active inquiry as an exercise, however, you show that you have a process to help clients solve their problems. You aren't just asking a random set of questions but rather you know what you are doing. Finally, by asking permission to move into active inquiry, you confirm that the client is coachable.

Third, dive into active inquiry, which is the meat of the process. You ask open-ended questions to produce results. A good open-ended question begins with a "what," "who," "where," "when," or "how" and perhaps a smattering of "why" (if too many, you come across as judgmental or interrogative).

You focus on asking primarily open-ended questions and not yes/no questions because you want to know what the client is thinking. You want to understand the client's world view. Yes/no questions tend to close off the conversation, especially if the client's answer is "no." Watch out for questions that jump to such suggestions as "Have you tried Y?" or that clarify the past, such as "Did you do X?" Develop the skill of letting clients arrive at their own insights and conclusions. Open-ended questions do that more effectively.

At the same time, yes/no or closed-ended questions can occasionally be very effective. A closed-ended question can be provocative or stand out as an exclamation point. For instance, "Would you rather be popular or successful?" The number of effective open-ended questions is nearly infinite. You will read about many of them as the book progresses to some specific coaching situations. To get started, here are some examples:

- What are your ideas to solve the problem?
- If you had to make a decision now, what would you do?
- Where do you want to start to start making progress?
- What lessons can you apply from a time when you successfully dealt with a challenge like this before?
- Who can you go to for support?
- What strengths can you bring to bear on this problem?

- If you were giving advice to a colleague with this issue, what would you tell them?
- What resources do you control that can help?
- Who do you need to influence to make progress here?
- What do you see as the root cause of the issue?
- If you were in my shoes, what would you want me to ask you?
- What is the other person's perspective on this issue?

Good open-ended questions have a certain amount of voltage to them. You're not just sitting in a coffee shop and talking about how the client's day is going. You are doing your best to help that person improve. You don't have to spend the client's time getting up to speed on the situation or being trained by this individual. You don't have to delve into the past unless it is to discover other situations that can help resolve the current one. Focus on assisting the client to gain insights and direction and for discovering the best approach to solving their challenge.

Many leaders wonder why they can't just jump in and tell the client what they would do. You can, but that's something different from coaching. Also, if you want people you are coaching to develop professionally and personally, it is most effective to let them solve their own problems.

A metaphor that helps explain this is to imagine that your client is a steam boiler filled to the top with steam. Most successful managers and leaders are confident and sometimes a little arrogant. They already know the answer. Their tendency is to resist suggestions made by others. Active inquiry allows the steam to vent by giving clients the opportunity to share their thoughts. Once the steam vents, the steam boiler empties out. It has room for more steam, meaning that the client is more likely to be open to suggestions and ideas from others.

During this phase of active inquiry, your primary job as a coach is to listen. Ideally, you are talking 25 percent of the time or less, while the client talks 75 percent of the time. From time to time, reflect on what you have heard—both the content of what the client says and any emotions you hear—to be sure you are talking about the same thing. In this way, active listening becomes the key to effective active inquiry and coaching. As a colleague of mine keeps reminding me, "If you listen, the client tells you the next question to ask."

Sometimes clients say they have no idea and want you to jump in with what you would do. Resist the urge to be the hero. Tell them that you have some ideas but want to hear their thinking first. After being a coach for almost two decades, I can almost guarantee that when clients ask for your ideas too soon they are setting you up. Every time I have opened my big mouth with my brilliant ideas, the client has argued with me that my ideas are wrong. If you do step in with your ideas and the client rejects them, that gives you the opportunity to say, "Well, you asked for my ideas. I gave them to you, and you didn't like them. Your turn! What are your ideas?"

Fourth is to wrap up. Do this by asking what insights your client has had and, if appropriate and with permission, offering your own observations. This phase begins when the conversation loses energy, or when it feels it's appropriate to summarize. At this point, simply say, "Let's pause here. What insight or insights, if any, have you had so far?" Let clients tell you what, if any, insights they have had. Then make sure you heard them and ask what they will do after the coaching session to take action. If appropriate, create a specific action plan and commitment by the client to take action. Challenge the client to agree to specific deadlines where it makes sense.

If you don't agree with the client's conclusions, ask permission to provide your perspective. Remember, however, that the client ultimately has to decide the right course for him or her. You are not a guru.

If you are aligned with the client's insights and you still have some observations of your own, ask permission to share them. Coaching is not a passive process, and clients usually want to hear your suggestions. You might say, "Do you mind if I share an observation?" Then, if the client is open to it, share it and find out what the client thinks about it. Don't just let it hang out there and end the session abruptly, as I have observed some coaches do.

At the end of the session, ask clients what was most valuable for them. Doing this is a great way to end the session and confirm whether or not you achieved the session's intent.

This process can take five minutes, thirty minutes, or an hour. Generally, the coach and client weave in and out of these steps during the course of a coaching session. Start with a goal, move into active inquiry, summarize and confirm any insights, and then keep moving ahead through active inquiry.

The best way to learn how to do active inquiry is by doing it. Coaching is a practice. Find some friends and colleagues, ask them about an issue they are facing, and ask permission to practice active inquiry with them. Work hard at listening, asking open-ended questions, and not jumping in to solve their problems. At some point, if you join a coach training program, such as the Center for Executive Coaching, you can even have your coaching conversations reviewed confidentially so that you keep getting better. Regardless, ask your client for advice about what you did well and what you could have done better.

Later on, you will read about an in-depth coaching process. For now, if you can lead active inquiry, you can coach. The flow of a session is quite simple, and consists of eight steps. Part of this was covered in the previous section.

The eight steps to conduct a single coaching session are:

1. Get clear with the client about the intent of the session.

2. Explain the active inquiry process and ask permission to dive in.

3. Use active inquiry to help the client improve.

4. Ask the client what insights they are having, confirm that the client is moving toward the intent of the session, and then get back to active inquiry.

5. Confirm next steps and what the client is accountable for doing. If and when appropriate, ask permission to share your own observations and insights, and get the client's feedback.

6. Schedule the next meeting or time to check in to follow up.

7. Ask the client what was most valuable from the coaching.

8. Confirm that you achieved the desired intent of the session.

There is no correct answer about how long a coaching session should be. For external coaches, sessions run between thirty and sixty minutes. If you are a manager, you might be able to coach a colleague or employee through an issue in a matter of minutes. On the other hand, sometimes an issue is so complex that it requires several sessions to tease out and resolve.

If you can run a single coaching session and make progress, you can set up multisession coaching engagements. Simply take small steps toward helping the client achieve their goals and keep getting better.

The Six Most Important Questions to Ask in a Coaching Session

One: "What would be the most valuable outcome you can achieve in our session?" This question focuses the session on a specific outcome. If the client doesn't have a clear, measurable, specific outcome, the session is unlikely to go anywhere. Even if clients simply wants a sounding board to check the wisdom of their idea about an issue, that at least tells you both what the client wants out of the session. Alternative wording is: "What outcome would make this session the most valuable hour of your week?"

Two: "What are your ideas to find a solution?" By asking this question, you jump right to the client's perceptions rather than interrupting with your own. Alternatives include "Where do you want to start?" and "What do you see as the key areas to discuss?" Frame the question to come from the highest and broadest level of logic to learn the most you can about the client's own thoughts about the issue.

Three: "What are your insights so far?" Ask this question after conducting some active inquiry. It will stimulate the discussion and help clients crystallize their thinking. Listen for how closely the client is to making progress on their stated outcome.

Four: "What would you like to discuss now?" Use this question to let the client guide the process. You learn more about clients when you let them guide the process instead of when you direct it with your questions.

Similarly, if the client is at a fork in the road and has brought up a few issues or points, you can summarize them and ask, "Which of these - or perhaps another avenue - do you want to discuss now?"

Five: "What are next steps?" By asking this question at the end of the session, the client has accountability to take action and keep making progress.

Six: "What was most valuable for you in our discussion?" Finally, this question adds value to your coaching. Listen for how closely you came to achieving the client's intent during the session, but sometimes the client gets value that is different from what was expected. Check to be sure that clients received what they wanted. If not, get back to active inquiry either now or by scheduling a future meeting.

Bad Coaching

Sometimes the best way to learn how to do something is by learning how not to do it. With that idea in mind, this article shares 14 examples of bad coaching. As you probably already know, coaching is partly the process of asking powerful questions to help the client deal with a challenge and improve. The coach works in partnership with the client to concentrate on certain issues, being focused, attentive, and reflecting back what has been heard. The coach offers suggestions only as a last resort and only with permission. In normal coaching conversations, the coach talks no more than 25 percent of the time. In contrast, here are examples of what not to do:

Fixing. If you are in a position to coach someone, you likely have experience and knowledge. You are also probably accustomed to stepping in and solving problems for people. When coaching, it can be extremely tempting to just give the client the answer, but when you jump right into solving the client's problem for them, you aren't coaching them. You could be advising, directing, teaching, or telling, but you aren't coaching.

The problem with fixing the client's problem is that just because you know the answer and would be able to implement it doesn't mean your client can. Coaching allows you to explore the best answer given where the client is right now along with their own unique talents, experiences, and style. The right solution for you might not be the right solution for the client. At the same time, even if your solution is correct, that doesn't mean your client is ready to implement it. Coaching allows you and the client to explore what challenges they face ahead.

What if you can't focus on the coaching because you are so sure you know the answer? If you are really certain that you are smart enough to know the right answer for the client, I suggest saying, "Do you mind if I jump in? I have a lot of experience with this issue, and I think I have a possible solution . . ." Share your idea, but let the client decide if they are ready to accept it. Then decide if you should continue being a consultant and advisor or if you should get back to being a coach. The latter means that you once again ask open-ended questions based on what the client wants to do. The former means that you use facts and logic to keep making your case. Be explicit with the client whether you are wearing the hat of a consultant, teacher, manager, or coach. Otherwise, your client might get confused.

I used to see myself as a smart guy who could solve any problems. I left coaching sessions feeling great about myself, but clients didn't implement my suggestions. When I allowed clients to solve their own problems, however, they felt smart and also felt that I was providing great value. *Don't fix. Coach.*

Knowing the answer and manipulating. If you know the answer, don't torture the client into figuring it out on their own with a series of Socratic questions. That's not coaching. At best, it is teaching the way they do in law school. At worst, it's manipulation—your attempt to get the client to come to the same conclusion as you have about a decision. From the client's point of view, it can feel condescending, tedious, and obnoxious to have to endure a series of questions knowing that the coach already has the answer.

Coaching is for situations when you and the client jump into the unknown. Don't play the game called "What's in my pocket?" If you already know the answer you want the person to also know, and you are not flexible about it, don't torture them. Simply tell them.

I worked with one manager who had a tendency to play this game. After interviewing his employees, I discovered that they called this manager's process "torturous self-realization." They loved his coaching style when it made sense for him to coach them, but when he already knew the answer, his employees found his approach to be inauthentic, tedious, and an inefficient use of time.

Interrupting. Don't interrupt when you coach. This deceptively simple rule can be hard for coaches who process information quickly. If you interrupt, you might cut off the client just when they are about to say something crucial. Get comfortable with silence. Wait a beat or two to be sure your client has finished speaking. Sometimes silence is the best coaching question of all because it encourages the client to think more deeply about the issue and go beyond the usual.

Distracted coaching. If you are in a noisy place, have crises to handle, are on the phone, or checking your email on your laptop, you are not in a position to coach. Coaching requires focus. Also, your clients deserve your attention. Don't coach when you are distracted.

Stacking questions. Stacking questions means that you ask your client more than one question at a time. For instance: "Tell me about the people involved in this issue. Also, what do you see as the main ways to resolve the issue? And, when you do resolve it, what are your action steps?" Even though the coach might be thinking of many different questions, a client can usually focus on, let alone remember, only one question at a time. Be patient. Let the process unfold. Ask one question at a time. If you do, you might also find that the next logical question is different from you had expected.

Checklist coaching. Checklist coaching means that you already have a list of questions to ask. There is no need to listen and no room for creativity or flexibility. Sometimes coaches falling into this habit don't even seem to be listening to the client. They ask one question, maybe grunt acknowledgment, and then move to the next. The client doesn't feel heard. The coach is more like a journalist conducting an interview than a coach. Instead, let the coaching process unfold naturally. Ask questions based on what you hear the client tell you. If the client doesn't seem to know what to say, you might introduce a different line of inquiry to ignite new ideas, but avoid rote, checklist-based coaching.

The Diagnostic. The diagnostic sounds like this: "Have you tried A? Have you tried B? Have you tried C? Have you tried D?" It's similar to having an algorithm or flow chart and similar to a doctor trying to diagnose a disease. This kind of approach is good for solving problems and for consulting, but it is not good coaching—good coaching asks open-ended questions and allows the client to come up with their own ideas. If you think a particular situation warrants a diagnostic approach, let clients know this is what you are doing so that they don't expect coaching.

Hiding suggestions. Some coaches hide their ideas in the form of a question, thinking that asking any type of question is good coaching. For instance:

"Have you tried X?"
"What about trying Y?"
"When will you set up a meeting with him to discuss this?"

It is better to be less directive and to ask questions that let clients lead the process. For instance:

"What are your ideas to solve this challenge?"
"What can you try?"
"Who can help?"

Bringing up some sort of fad book or trend. Some coaches are suckers for the latest trend or fad. Whether it is taking emotional intelligence far beyond where the initial author intended, claiming pseudoscientific applications of neuroscience, becoming a fan of the latest approach to personal transformation, or glomming on to the latest positive psychology guru, you can bet there are coaches waiting in line to share it with clients. These coaches come across more as evangelists pushing a particular philosophy. They make the coaching profession seem flaky. Worse, prospects view these coaches the same way we think about religious evangelists who knock on our doors on Sundays. We want them to go away.

Don't look for fads. Let the client's problem dictate your approach instead of pushing an approach and hoping it solves a problem for the client. Ask great questions, listen, and focus on the client's specific situation rather than forcing the client into a specific box. Applying frameworks or concepts from various disciplines can be valuable, but wait until the client's situation calls for it.

Never-ending, open-ended questions. Some coaches believe you can never offer advice or observations to a client. They insist on only asking open-ended questions. As a result, their coaching feels more like therapy. It also becomes frustrating. One executive who came to me for coaching after firing a coach who did this called this form of coaching "an expensive waste of time."

A balance exists between jumping too quickly to suggesting solutions and not offering observations or insights at all. It is perfectly acceptable to offer your ideas and insights. In fact, clients expect it. If you wait until you have thoroughly explored the client's issue and possible solutions from their point of view and then ask permission to share your insights, the client usually appreciates it.

Caring more than they do and getting frustrated. Sometimes it feels that you care more about the client's goals and aspirations than the client does. They simply won't do what they need to do to achieve the goals they claim they want to achieve. It's frustrating to feel this way.

Many parents also face this issue, for instance, when their child declares they want to go to Harvard, yet won't do their homework. When this happens, avoid the temptation of getting too attached to your client's goals and becoming disappointed.

You can certainly talk openly about the client's lack of effort and coach them about what might be going on to prevent the required actions, but if you start judging the client, become exasperated, or even chide them during coaching sessions, you have jumped into the realm of bad coaching.

Getting trained on the client's time. You can coach a client without being an expert in their field or even about the situation they are facing. If you find you are asking clients to bring you up to speed on key terminology, how to do their job, or in-depth play-by-play about what happened recently, you might be doing things that are valuable to you but meaningless to the client. These types of questions are called situational questions. A few can be helpful in the way a bit of salt can enhance a meal, but you are not helping anyone if you get carried away.

One of the powerful aspects of coaching is that you don't have to have content knowledge to ask the kinds of questions that help the client improve. This statement might not make sense right now, but you will discover it is accurate the more you coach. Once you realize this, coaching becomes easier, more fun, and more effective.

Doing the client's dirty work What do you do if the client asks you to coach employees who are not performing as they should? One option is to go and coach them, but be careful. Sometimes clients ask the coach to step in and coach members of their team when what they really want is for you to do their dirty work for them. It is often better to coach your clients on how they can be more effective in leading and influencing the other person.

For instance, I worked with a client who was leading a major performance improvement program. He asked me to talk to one of his executives who wasn't participating in the program and coach him to get on board and find opportunities to improve productivity in his area. What would you do in that situation? In my judgment, my client wasn't asking me to coach this executive. He was asking me to influence the executive to get on board with the program. That's my client's job! On further exploration, I learned that my client was a bit afraid of this executive and didn't like confronting him. So we worked on strategies for my client to get over this fear and how best to influence this executive

Remember: Coaching isn't about stepping in and doing a client's work. It is about helping clients be more effective so that they can do the work without you.

Failing to put in place ways to track progress and measure results. Like any other profession, coaching is about getting results. If you don't agree on a clear intent and outcome with your client, you won't know if you deliver value. If you don't put a way to measure progress in place, you won't know how your client is doing. If you don't track progress, you won't know when you have achieved the desired outcome(s). Any subject for coaching – from improved confidence to new attitudes and behaviors, stronger relationships, and better individual or team performance – and be measured if the coach and client are thoughtful enough.

Find Your Coaching Style

If you are a manager, you know that different leadership and communication styles work better with different people and in different situations. The same is true for coaching. Most seasoned coaches adapt to the situation and needs of the client. At the same time, almost all coaches have a natural style that fits them best. A few adjectives that define different coaching styles include edgy, nurturing, contemplative, patient, intuitive, positive, intense, high-energy, relaxed, logical, visionary, provocative, and peaceful. One way to define your style is by looking at how you balance ego, results, and relationships.

First, coaches need some degree of ego to be on equal footing with highly successful managers, executives, and up-and-coming talent. The coach who emphasizes ego a bit too much, however, comes across as arrogant and might have trouble stepping back and letting the client do the work.

Second, coaching is meaningless if the coach and client don't achieve results. Meanwhile, the coach who overemphasizes results tends to come across as too forceful and directive, even to the point of hurting relationships.

Third, the coach and client should have trust, rapport, and a strong working relationship. Otherwise, the client won't open up and be willing to be vulnerable. On the other hand, the coach who emphasizes relationships too much might not say what needs to be said to get results. That coach might be more interested in being popular than in helping the client with open, honest conversation.

Different situations, organizational cultures, and clients call for a different balance of these three attributes. For instance, a coach working with a Wall Street CEO might need a different style than a coach who works with an up-and-coming manager in a small nonprofit organization. Even with a natural style, the savvy coach adjusts to the client and situation. For instance, I had the opportunity to interview one of the most successful college basketball coaches in NCAA history. When I asked him how he coached individuals on the team, he replied that in general there are three types of players. The first wants the coach who puts his arm around the player's shoulder. The second responds best to tough love, or what this coach called "kick in the pants coaching." The third type does best when the coach calls the player's mom. His job as a coach is to get to know his players and adapt his style accordingly.

What about you? What is your natural style as a coach? Do you prefer to tell it like it is and be a bit forceful? Do you set a completely positive tone and emphasize what's working well? Do you step back and try for a neutral tone? There is no right or wrong answer, but the more you can adapt your style to what's right for the situation, the more effective your coaching will be.

Suppose your client has just gotten some negative feedback about a project they are leading. Because of this feedback, they are feeling down. Depending on the client, this is probably not be the best time to get on the client's case and reinforce the negative feedback. It's probably better just to listen, let the client vent, and perhaps help the client talk about what's working well and how they can use their talents to get back on track.

Similarly, what style would you use if your client has failed to follow through with an action plan for a few weeks in a row? Let's assume you have already explored some of the underlying reasons why the client won't act, and the client told you they had resolved those. Perhaps it is time to add a bit more edge to your coaching style, maybe even questioning whether or not the client is really committed to achieving their stated goals.

Another way to adapt your style is by completing an off-the-shelf assessment of your client. A validated, reliable assessment tool will give you insights about your client's natural thinking style, communication style, behavioral traits, and even values. For example, if you know that someone is more direct and bottom line in their thinking and communication, you would coach them differently from somebody who needs to go into minute, step-by-step detail about issues. Similarly, you might move at a different pace with a client who processes information very quickly compared with a client who needs time to process information.

External coaches have a bit of an advantage compared with internal managers who use coaching as a tool to develop their people because they can build a brand based on their natural and unique style. They become known for solving specific issues in specific ways. They can attract clients that are comfortable with their style and approach. In contrast, managers inherit a diverse group of employees and colleagues. They can't choose their coaching clients the way that external coaches can and have to be more flexible.

Take a moment to define your natural style as a coach. What types of people seem most comfortable for you? Which types of people would be more challenging? In which situations or with which people do you see yourself needing to adapt? Finally, how willing are you to adapt and be more flexible depending on the situation and the individual?

The Sublime Art of Asking One Question that Changes Everything

The best coaches do less, not more. The more you talk, the less you learn about a client and how that person is thinking about challenges they face. The more you step in and solve the client's problem, the less you allow the client to develop. Coaching is about building capacity and developing people, not about showing how much you know. Consider the ideal of finding just one question to ask during a coaching session - a question that somehow changes everything for the client.

Perhaps you have had the good fortune of being in a meeting with an executive who had a similar gift. That person patiently listens to all the points of view in the room and then asks a simple question that changes the way everyone thinks about the issue. Something like this happened in the carbonated beverage industry and changed the entire vision, strategy, and conversation among its biggest competitors. Imagine a strategic planning meeting at one of the biggest companies in the industry. As usual, everyone is talking about how the company can increase share of market among carbonated soft drinks. Suddenly, someone asks, "What would be a different way to think about market share than share of beverages sold?"

This simple question led to a massive insight: "What if we stop thinking about share of the carbonated beverage market and think about share of stomach?" Now the people around the table see the opportunity to sell other beverages, such as sports drinks, fruit juice, and bottled water. They also see the possibility of marketing snack foods, restaurants, and anything else related to food and beverage consumption. The entire focus of the company - and soon the industry - expands dramatically, as does its growth potential. One question changes everything.

As a coach, unlike with this example, you don't have to come up with earth-shattering questions every coaching session or even every engagement. The idea of asking one question that changes everything is ideal, but it's not possible to do this all the time. Not every coaching session has major breakthroughs or cathartic moments, but the concept of one-question-coaching is a good one to keep in mind to make sure you are focused on listening and asking questions that bring high impact and value to the person you are coaching. The best coaching questions are often the simplest, such as the six key questions described in an earlier chapter. Even asking clients for their ideas to solve a problem can open up possibilities.

As you practice coaching, think before you ask a question. Consider if it will be beneficial for your client. Does your question have a little bit of voltage to it so that it gets the client thinking? Does it allow the client to see new possibilities, see things in a new way, and at least move on to insights and action? By thinking about these questions, you are on the path to the idea of asking one question that changes everything.

Getting Beyond
the What and the How

Some coaches worry that they can't coach people without significant content knowledge. For instance, what if you don't have an MBA? What if you don't have clinical experience and are asked to coach physicians or nurse managers. Most organizations have many people who are thoroughly familiar with highly technical content. They also have more than enough people who can develop action plans and process maps. Even still, they don't execute or get things done. How can this be when organizations invest so much in people with the right education and training?

It's because a third aspect is involved in getting results beyond the "what" and the "how." It is often invisible to leaders and managers, especially in highly technical organizations. The third aspect involves looking below the surface:

- how leaders or managers appear to others
- the impact they have when communicating
- how they build and nurture relationships up, down, and across the organization
- how well they navigate the politics of the organization
- how effectively they engage and mobilize people
- how they resolve conflict
- how aware they are of other people's styles, motivations, and values - and adapts to them or not

- their perceptions and thinking style and how these ei[...]
  them ahead or hold them back

- their natural filters and orientations when making decisions

- how they lead and work on teams

- how they react to change

- the conversations they have and don't have

- how they carry themselves in high-pressure situations

- how and with whom they spend their time

- what they reward and what they punish

- how they influence others

The above attributes are only a few of the areas where a coach goes beyond the what and the how. Coaching is powerful and valuable because the coach sees things in the spaces between analyzing and planning. Coaching is able to uncover the issues that keep organizations with top talent from getting things done and being as effective as they can be. As a coach, you have the opportunity to focus your discussions on areas where most leaders, managers, and up-and-coming talent don't spend enough time.

This focus on the third, unseen domain has two sides to it. On the one side, some leaders question the value of coaching. They see it as soft. The areas that coaching explores weren't part of their years of training, and by extension, aren't relevant. On the other side, once you can demonstrate the ability to use coaching to get better results, you will earn the respect and admiration of your clients.

Ethics and Confidentiality

As with any profession, coaching has developed a set of ethical guidelines. The International Coach Federation has one of the most detailed, and you can visit their website to read them. Generally, the guidelines state what you would expect and are straightforward:

- Don't misrepresent your credentials as a coach.
- Disclose conflicts of interest and avoid coaching engagements that have significant conflicts of interest.
- Set up a clear contract with the client.
- Don't get romantically involved with your clients.
- If the client wants to end the coaching relationship, let him.
- Maintain confidentiality.

The last one deserves discussion. The first coach I ever had burned me badly by breaking confidentiality. At the time, I reported to the CEO of the company and was having a conflict with him. I assumed that everything we said in our coaching sessions was confidential, but the coach blabbed some of my more candid thoughts about the CEO to him directly, which caused serious damage to our relationship.

Coaching works best when it is confidential. Otherwise, the client won't be as willing to open up to you. Unless clients share that they are thinking of hurting themselves or others or that they are doing something illegal, you should not tell anyone else. Not his manager. Not Human Resources.

If coaching works, the results should speak for themselves. No one other than you and the client need to see the sausage being made. Even if clients share they are looking for another job or thinking about starting a company, that should remain confidential. The vast majority of employees are looking for another job and/or thinking about starting a company! You don't have to snitch on them. Ditto if the client talks negatively about colleagues. Who doesn't feel negatively about their colleagues from time to time?

When you set up a coaching relationship, if you don't want to hear certain things from the client, such as the fact that they are actively searching for a new job, let them know up front. Don't set them up to regret the coaching relationship later on. Confidentiality gets tricky when the person you are coaching is also reporting to you. In that case, you have to make it clear about when the conversation is truly off the record and when it is on the record and can be used in performance reviews or promotion decisions. If you don't feel comfortable or able to put up a wall between these two domains, then be sure the employee knows you will treat the coaching conversation as any other discussion between you.

I will never forget the sting of that coach when she violated confidentiality with me. Please don't give your coaching clients a similar experience.

The Attitudes of the Coach

A significant part of being a coach is how you show up to clients. How you show up has a lot to do with your attitudes or orientations. If you have the right orientations and are competent with coaching skills, your clients will be delighted. Shown below are a few attitudes that define how the effective coach appears.

Be curious. Come into coaching conversations without knowing everything. Instead, put your judgments aside and be curious. Learn as much as you can about how clients think about their situation. Before you jump in and fix things, discover how the client would solve a challenge. Ask questions and listen. Let the client be the smartest person in the room. Being curious while not needing to know the answers is a powerful attitude to have in coaching, career, and life.

Have a dialogue. Coaching is a dialogue between two people. Together, you are working to help the client have insights and move to a new, more effective place. Don't tell. Don't teach. Don't fix. Yes, you can offer your insights and observations, but be patient and wait until you have explored the client's view in depth. As noted earlier, try to speak less than 25 percent of the coaching session.

Balance ego, results, and relationships. When a previous chapter invited you to better understand your natural coaching style, we discussed the importance of balancing ego, results, and relationships. It is worth repeating this principle. With each client, in each situation, find that balance. If you push too hard, the client might get results (or at least agree to do what you want during the session), but you will damage the relationship. If you don't push hard enough, you might preserve the relationship, but the client won't get results, and, of course, the relationship will suffer, too, because it is inauthentic. If the coaching session is too much about you and how smart and successful you are, both results and relationships suffer. Find that balance during every coaching conversation.

Be open and honest. The effective coach is on equal footing with clients and is comfortable having open and honest conversations. If clients don't do what they said they would do between sessions, the coach mentions that and asks permission to explore why the client is being accountable. If the coach observes a behavior that might be hurting the client's effectiveness and ability to achieve stated goals, that is mentioned, and the coach asks permission to discuss it. The coach feels comfortable saying what needs to be said—all while still balancing ego, results, and relationships.

Empathize. Coaches not only listen to what the client is saying but also empathize with how the client is feeling.

See possibility. When clients are stuck, mired in complaints and negativity, the effective coach creates a sense of possibility. The coach is not unrealistic about what is possible, but that person's way of speaking and acting encourages clients to keep pushing forward in the face of uncertainty and difficult challenges.

Stand for the client's aspirations and potential. The coach is a stake in the ground for what clients can be and do. That's who the coach is. If the client wavers, thinks too small, or has doubt, the coach does not because the coach represents his or her aspirations and potential. The coach represents the client's most ambitious, noble, and inspiring goals. If needed, the coach challenges clients, reminding them of their goals and providing a little push to keep them moving in the right direction.

Sometimes doing this can be challenging because coaches might feel they care more about the client's aspirations and sees more potential for the client than the client does. In this case, the coach is open and honest and expresses concerns while also staying positive and emphasizing what's possible.

Build capacity. The coach is not working with the client just to get it done. Rather, the coach wants to help clients improve their capabilities and performance over the long term. Coaches don't step in and just do it. Instead, they detach themselves just enough to let the client determine the best course of action while developing professionally.

All of the above attitudes are connected like pearls on a necklace. You can't practice one without practicing all of them. Which of these strengths do you have? Which are more challenging? Your answer might change from client to client.

Here is a piece of advice to strengthen client relationships: Before a coaching session, take a moment to get grounded in each of these attitudes. Ask yourself which attitudes are strong, and which might be missing or weak in your relationship with the client. Commit to maintaining or building on what is working and improving what is missing or weak. After the coaching session, take a moment to reflect on how the session went. Go through the same process so that you remain grounded in these attitudes and keep strengthening your ability to show up as representing them.

Finally, if you had to build your own list of attitudes, what would you add, delete, or edit? The above list works for me and many other coaches but may not be perfect for you. Give some thought to the list you would create, and continue trying to keep getting stronger in those attitudes.

Part Two

THE COACHING PROCESS

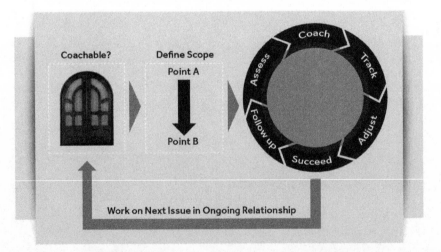

Overview of the Coaching Process

I f you plan on coaching somebody for more than a single session, you should follow a more detailed coaching process. Seven steps are involved in the process diagrammed above. Here is a brief description of each step followed by more details.

Be sure that coachability is in place. Without coachability, the entire coaching process shuts down. Coachability means that your client has given permission for coaching to take place.

Define goals, scope, and contract. Set a clear goal or goals with the client. Then agree on the scope and boundaries of the coaching relationship.

Assess. Take time to understand the root causes of the client's challenge. Get the data you and the client need to develop the most effective and efficient coaching plan.

Coach, track, and adjust. Most of the coaching process is about coaching, tracking progress, and adjusting as needed on the way to helping clients achieve their goals.

Succeed and celebrate. In today's organizations, few leaders or managers take the time to celebrate and acknowledge results. In the coaching process, take time to step back and acknowledge achievements as they happen.

Work on the next issue. Coaching is about having a long-term relationship with the client. As the client achieves one goal, identify the next challenge. Every single leader and manager has room to keep growing.

Follow up. Sometimes clients slip, even after achieving initial success. Build in time to follow up with the client and make sure that everything remains on course and results are sustained.

Let's now look at each step in more depth.

Confirm and Establish Coachability

You can't coach somebody who isn't coachable. Being coachable means being receptive to advice, trying out new ideas, and listening to tough feedback. For this reason, establishing coachability is not only the start of the coaching process but also the gateway to effective coaching. Anytime that coachability does not exist, the coaching process shuts down. Many executives are not particularly coachable. They think they already know or can figure it out. Some need to be in LOTS of pain before they ask for, or take, anybody else's counsel. As a coach, it is your job to create a coachable environment between you and your clients.

As I write this, a show called *Trading Spouses* is on television. In this show, two wives switch families for a while. During tonight's episode, one of the wives is a professional motivational speaker. When she goes to her new family, she naturally begins "motivating" them just as she does with her real family. How do you think her new family reacts? They want to kick her out. The family isn't receptive to her ideas. They are not coachable, at least not by her. They are not coachable because they don't think they have a problem and because they haven't agreed to be coached by her. They don't know her, are still getting used to having a stranger in their home, and certainly haven't asked for her ongoing opinions. This woman started coaching her new family without creating an environment conducive to the reception of her advice.

Nobody wants unsolicited advice. Lots of people don't even want advice when they ask for it (i.e., "Does this dress make me look fat?"). Yet, many of us love giving unsolicited advice. We intervene without permission. In personal situations, this behavior is called "nagging."

Don't assume your client is coachable simply because they have asked you for coaching. Coachability is a mind-set that comes and goes, much like the tides. Every time you sit down with a client, you have to be sure that he or she is coachable. You can do this in three ways:

First, the client can ask for coaching by requesting your opinion or counsel. In this case, if you have tough advice to deliver, you should let the client know and confirm they are receptive.

Second, you can ask permission. For example, "Joe, I've listened to what you have to say about the situation and have some ideas, but first I want to be sure you are open to hearing some tough advice."

Third, if the client seems to be resisting your input, you can be assertive. "Joe, you said you were open to my coaching. I don't mind if you have logical issues with what we are discussing, but it seems like you are not even giving the coaching a chance. I need you to be more coachable. At least take a moment to consider some of the questions I am asking."

You should constantly be assessing your clients and your relationship with them to be sure they are coachable. If they are not, stop the session and re-create a coachable environment. When a client isn't coachable, there are two possible reasons why:

First, it could be the client, who might be distracted, or who might have a more urgent issue to discuss. The client could also be feeling too vulnerable.

Second, it could be you. Maybe you are pushing too hard or not hard enough. Perhaps you are not listening well. You might be directing the conversation where the client doesn't want to go.

Start by pointing the finger at yourself before you blame the client.

Consider different approaches. Talk openly with the client. Executives and managers are by nature a challenging group. They aren't going to simply sit back and allow you to pronounce your findings. They will want to go back and forth with you and eventually arrive at their own conclusions. Some might want you to serve as a "sparring partner" (as one of my clients calls me), so they will push back. You constantly have to earn the right to be their coach. None of this means that your clients are uncoachable. It simply means that they are smart, thoughtful individuals. Therefore, you should not claim that your client is uncoachable too quickly.

On the other hand, if you do get a client who is truly uncoachable, after an appropriate amount of discussion and chances to get back on track, you might have no choice but to terminate the coaching agreement.

In other words, you constantly have to balance two tensions with clients. On the one hand, you have to stay on your toes, provide value through coaching, and earn their respect. On the other hand, you also have to make sure your clients are open to coaching, open to hearing uncomfortable advice, and open to new ideas that may take them out of their comfort zone.

Set the Foundation for a Successful Engagement

Define Goals, Scope, and Boundaries

This step has two parts. First, define what would constitute a successful engagement for your client. In fact, the first question any coach should ask a client is: "What would a successful coaching relationship achieve for you?" Even better, ask: "What would make this engagement the best and most valuable career development experience of your life?" Your job is to get specific, measurable results for your client. Start every engagement by defining those results. A well-defined outcome is:

Measurable. You can prove that you got the results through metrics. Different situations call for different approaches. For instance, if clients want to change a behavior, you should be prepared to interview their colleagues over time to find out how often they observed the old and new behavior(s) in question. Likewise, if the client wants to improve the way he or she spends time, then you should measure how s/he spends time as your coaching engagement progresses.

Specific. "Specific" means that you are getting finite, concrete results. "I want to feel better" is not specific; "I want to increase sales in my department by 25%, from $10 million to $12.5 million" is specific

Time bound. A good outcome definition includes a deadline. Without a deadline, there is no accountability. "Someday" is not a deadline. "By January 31 of this year" is a deadline. Work with your client to define aggressive but specific and measurable results, with a deadline. Once you do, you will notice a gap between where the client is and where the client wants to be. In the above example related to sales, the gap is $2.5 million (let's say the deadline is within twelve months). It will be helpful to your coaching work to define that gap. When you begin the assessment phase, you can then develop a structured, logical process for understanding the root cause of the gap and how to move quickly to the client's desired future state.

The second piece of the coaching foundation is setting scope and boundaries, or contracting. On any engagement, it is essential for you to be clear about the scope and boundaries of your work. What will and won't the engagement cover? What types of subjects are within bounds and out of bounds? When is the engagement done? What are the ground rules for this engagement? These and other critical questions are important to answer up front and often throughout the engagement.

The following are some of the key scope-related questions to discuss with a client before an engagement begins. Don't simply ask the questions that follow and expect your client to answer them. Have your own suggestions ready to propose.

Scope

How often do we meet, and for how long? A coaching engagement can range from a couple of sessions to a year or more. Meeting frequency can vary from once per week to every other week, monthly, or even quarterly once the client gets traction and just needs to check in occasionally. Work with your client to determine the best duration and frequency. If in doubt, start with weekly meetings and adjust from there. Also, I have found that it is hard to see sustainable results with anything less than a three-month commitment, and I usually won't coach a client for less than six months.

When does the engagement begin and end?

What kind of follow-up is included after the engagement ends? I build in at least one follow-up session after the formal coaching period ends, which allows me to check in with the client, address any remaining challenges, and be sure that the results from our coaching are sticking.

What kind of assessment will be done?

How many people will be interviewed (if there are interviews)?

Who will be interviewed and for how long?

How do we track results?

Who is involved in this engagement and who is not?

Who handles logistics of setting up any interviews?

Boundaries

What questions can be asked when conducting interviews and what questions or topics are out of bounds?

Is it okay to share findings with anyone else?

What kinds of topics are within bounds in discussions with the client and which are out of bounds (e.g., personal issues)?

What political land mines should I avoid when speaking to any colleagues or working with you?

Should interviews with your colleagues remain confidential? My preference is to allow what people say to be made public but to keep the identity of the person who says it confidential. At the same time, I agree to remove any comments that might reveal a specific individual.

What do I do if you don't keep your word or do any assignments that you agree to do?

What do I do if you don't seem to be coachable?

What happens if you have to cancel or reschedule a session? My policy is that the client agrees to give seventy-two hours' notice. Coaching is meant to be a privilege and a top priority.

In addition, I like to create a set of ground rules up front with my clients, starting with the following list:

The client agrees to be coachable. This includes listening to advice from colleagues and from the coach.

We will be open and honest with one another. This includes giving each other honest feedback and advice.

We will do our respective assignments on time.

We will eliminate distractions during our sessions in order to focus on our work. No cell phones, other calls, interruptions, or checking email while we work.

Everything the client says during sessions is to be kept in the strictest confidence.

As the engagement progresses, you and the client may find that you need to renegotiate the goals, scope, and boundaries, which is normal. Sometimes goals clients thought they had change. Sometimes the client has new priorities. Sometimes the coach or client notices a behavior that is getting in the way of the coaching and has to request a change. For instance, I once worked with a client who traveled all over the world. He started calling me on my cell phone during his business hours, which was sometimes the middle of the night for me. I requested that he either pay me more to answer my cell at all hours of the night, or that he call me during my business hours. He chose the latter.

Assess the Client/Situation, Diagnose, and Design

The assessment phase is critical for a successful engagement. This phase sheds light on how your clients can move from where they are to where they want to be. With a sound assessment, you can determine the best intervention(s) to help your clients improve. Some of your clients may not have the patience for a lengthy assessment phase. Some clients think they already know the answer, but you have every right to structure an assessment that gives you the information you need to help your client succeed.

At the same time, you have an obligation to be efficient during your assessment process. Many coaches (and consultants) are sloppy during their assessment. They do what the consulting firm McKinsey & Company calls "boiling the ocean." Like a doctor who orders every test imaginable, these coaches do all sorts of surveys, interviews, and analyses—almost by rote—and still don't necessarily gain many insights. The way to be efficient during your assessment is to structure your thinking about what might be causing your client's problem ahead of time. When you have a solid structure in place, it is easy to map out an efficient and effective assessment process. You can assess the client in the following ways:

Off-the-shelf assessments give insights about the client's thinking and communication styles, behavioral traits, values, career preferences, and other specific traits (e.g., response to conflict, energy level, relationship to change, and relationship to risk). You can choose from among many assessments on the market. Some are highly validated, while others are more like fortune cookies. Most coaches use at least one reliable assessment that helps clients have insights about their style and adapt to a specific situation. Examples range from the Myers-Briggs Type Inventory, DiSC, Birkman, Profiles International, and dozens more. If you use an assessment, be sure to get trained in how to use it properly, how to avoid misuse (e.g., not all assessments are legally allowed to be used to screen for employment), and the reliability and validity of the tool.

A 360-degree verbal assessment is a confidential assessment in which the coach interviews people up, down, across, and sometimes outside the organization. This is different from a 360-degree review, which goes through Human Resources and is used for performance reviews. During the 360 process, the coach asks people about the clients' strengths, what they can do better, and other advice appropriate for the client's situation. Done properly, the 360 is a confidential process that lets clients know how they come across to others—without giving away who said what. This is my favorite approach to assessing leaders and managers because I can get to know the client's colleagues and discover the real impact the client has with other people.

Active inquiry is a powerful conversation to work with the client to get to the root causes of a challenge.

Your own impressions can be useful to assess the client and the situation. Don't invalidate your own instincts. As long as you ask permission to share your impressions and the client is open to hearing them, the way the client comes across to you can be revealing.

The client's job description can help you be clear on their role and what they are expected to achieve, but be sure to probe more deeply about what people expect from your client and that might appear in the formal job description.

The organization's strategic plan can give you insights about the clients' key initiatives and how aligned they seem to be with the organization's mission, values, and priorities.

Performance reviews and the organization's competency models can provide important data about how clients are doing and the skills they have to develop.

The client's professional development plan, if they have one, will give you a clear picture of where the client wants to head in the organization and how they plan to get there. A good professional development plan includes short- and long-term career goals followed by the work experiences, relationships, new skills, education, and other activities that will achieve the goals. If clients don't have a development plan, you can create one with them. Doing this gives you the opportunity to hold the client accountable for achieving the plan, including talking with others in the organization to support them.

Observing the client in action, for instance, in a team meeting, can give valuable insights too. Does the client show up on time? What does the client's body language say to others? How much do clients say, and how much do they listen? How well do they include everyone? What is their style?

The assessment process can help a client be more engaged in the coaching process. For instance, assume you are working with a professional that has a reputation for being abrasive. Abrasive behavior is tolerated in many industries and companies, especially when the leader or manager is a superstar in other areas. A good example is in healthcare, where numerous physicians have been labeled abrasive or even disruptive once they switch from medical practice to more administrative duties. That's because many of them never had training about working in organizations or haven't learned that the behaviors that might work in a surgical suite or emergency room do not work well in a more administrative setting. Initially, physicians might not be open to the idea that their behavior in meetings with nonclinicians is ineffective. Their behavior might actually be a blind spot for them. When you complete a 360 verbal assessment, the client might say, "Yes, that is what they have told you, but they don't understand the pressures of being a physician. Most of the people you interviewed are nonclinicians, and they just don't get it."

Next, you might diplomatically tell the physician that based on a couple of sessions together you also notice that this person has some behaviors that could be perceived as abrasive. The client might reply, "So what? You are not a physician either."

Third, you might do a validated assessment. For instance, the ProfileXT puts clients on a bell curve that compares them to other people in similar positions so that clients can benchmark themselves on certain thinking styles and behavioral traits. The physician now has validated data that might show that this person is an extremely fast processor, has a high energy level, and is also not as accommodating or manageable as the individual's peers. This data, which is reliable and validated, and which adds a dimension to the previous feedback, might get the physician to start to notice a pattern.

Fourth, you might observe clients in a meeting and take notes when they roll their eyes, interrupt, or even leave the meeting early because they are bored.

Suddenly, you have enough data from different sources for the physician to recognize that there is a problem, and that it is in this person's best interests to work on some new behaviors. At the Center for Executive Coaching, we call this approach to assessments "nowhere-to-hide coaching."

Different situations call for different assessments. For instance, when two people have a conflict and want coaching to resolve it, I might assess by interviewing each person separately and doing an off-the-shelf assessment to get a sense of their different styles. I don't need to do a 360 verbal assessment of both of them or observe each in meetings. I can get the information I need with a simpler approach.

Once you have assessed a situation, your next step is to diagnose it and create a coaching plan to help your client get the desired results. Sometimes all you need to do is set up an action plan with your client and a way to check in to be sure that the client is taking action. Or you may need to develop a more in-depth and creative plan. As a coach, you are working with a relatively blank slate and have the freedom to develop a coaching agenda that you think will do the best job.

Coach, Track, Adjust

Your coaching work either moves toward results or it doesn't. If you find that you and the client are off track, make a midcourse correction. Client progress rarely follows a direct, linear path. If it did, your services would not be as valuable as they are because anybody could coach.

A fundamental requirement when coaching is that you find a way to track results, which you can do in many different ways. If the issue is a behavior that the client wants to change, you can have the client ask people to rate how often they see the new behavior in action. If the issue is about time management, clients can track their use of time and report back on productivity. If the client wants to be more influential, you and the client can identify situations for the client to influence people more effectively and track how successful they are at achieving their goals. If the issue is more feelings based, for instance, when the client lacks confidence or feels stress, you can have the client rate their confidence or stress levels at different times and track improvements. Even if the client simply wants a sounding board, you can still set goals each session for whether or not clarity has been achieved.

There is always a way to set goals and track. Without putting this kind of process into place, coaching has a tendency to meander and not provide clear value. Take 100% responsibility for the impact your coaching is having. If you and the client are not on track, determine how to get on track—without blaming the client or being a victim.

Succeed and Celebrate

When the client get results, whether by achieving a short-term milestone or by realizing the overall goal of the coaching process, acknowledge the results and celebrate with your client. Acknowledging and celebrating doesn't mean you have to throw a party. Many executives and managers are bottom-line, self-motivated people. For them, getting a result is rewarding in and of itself. Also, new behaviors usually lead to improved response from colleagues and better results, which is the best reward. Usually, it is enough for the coach to remind the client about the starting point, acknowledge what has been achieved so far, and confirm what these results mean to the client and that person's organization.

The easy part is for the coach to acknowledge results. The hard part is getting the client to do it. In many organizations, especially with driven and highly educated people, leaders and managers are pretty hard on themselves. They assume that when results happen they would have happened regardless of their contributions. This is where the coach can help them recognize their contribution. Aside from creating a positive environment, this part of the coaching process also helps clients get better at talking about their contributions and promoting themselves (appropriately) in their organizations.

Choose the Next Situation/Goal

A good coach keeps clients for life or at least for a very long time. After you achieve one goal with a client, the client should see the value that you bring. Clients who are coachable want to keep growing and getting better. Find something else to work on, and repeat the process. Sometimes clients want to move right into the next goal, and sometimes they want to take a break. Let the client guide you, but at the same time listen for new initiatives, challenges, and professional development opportunities where you can bring value.

Follow-up

The final part of the coaching process is the follow-up. Build follow-up sessions into your engagements with the client. By doing this, you make sure the client does not backtrack or let gains slip away. Also, for external coaches, follow-up sessions allow you to stay in touch with your clients and can lead to additional work and referrals. Finally, by following up, you show the client that unlike many professionals you don't just disappear when the real work begins.

For instance, I worked with a coaching firm that provided clients with a free "10,000 mile checkup." About three months after an engagement ended, we came back to assess ongoing performance and results. We could identify any obstacles to ongoing success and develop additional interventions to regain momentum and results. Of course, you can't follow up if you don't put a sound tracking and measurement system into place as part of your initial work. Be sure that you have metrics in place, and that your client continues to measure results after you are gone.

What Coaching Really Looks Like

O f all the professional services, coaching is one of the easiest to scope out and plan. It's not like we are creating the critical path for building a rocket ship or even developing a project plan for a team of software consultants. If you plan on coaching a client for more than a single session, the process is simple. All you have to do is choose how often to meet, agree on the questions we discussed about scope and boundaries, conduct any relevant assessments up front, and jump into coaching conversations that move the client toward their goal(s). If the goals change, adjust the coaching accordingly.

I typically meet with a client weekly at first and then every other week or even monthly as the client makes progress. Some coaches meet monthly from start to finish. I suggest setting a six-month engagement with clients. I'll go for three months to start if absolutely required but have found that it takes at least six months to make significant progress. Some coaches insist on a one-year contract for an executive and 18–24 months for a team or for the owner of a growing business to see measurable change.

Let's assume you are coaching a leader who wants to get better. I call this the leadership tune-up. A coaching plan might include the following:

- An introductory session to agree on goals and the rules of the road as well as to set up assessments.
- A week or so to complete the assessment(s).
- A meeting to review the assessments and agree on the coaching plan.

- Regular coaching sessions for achieving the goals of the engagement. During these sessions, we work toward the overall goal; discuss current issues, especially as the relate to the overall goal of the coaching; put into place a behavioral coaching process if appropriate; and introduce other topics related to leadership if time permits.

Built into the above process are regular check-ins to evaluate progress, measure results, and determine whether or not to meet more or less frequently.

Keep it simple!

Part Three

MORE COACHING CONVERSATIONS

Overview

We already introduced active inquiry, the most fundamental coaching conversation. While all coaching conversations could fit under the umbrella of active inquiry, additional conversations are worth knowing.

Setting goals and defining the problem. Coaching is ultimately about achieving results. It is much easier to achieve results if the coach has clear conversations with the client to set goals and define the problem.

Listening. If an effective coach speaks only 25 percent of the time, then what do coaches do during the remaining 75 percent? They listen. Listening as a coach is more than being present and reflecting on what the client is saying. Listening is an active process that helps the coach discover the best question to ask next.

Appreciative inquiry. This is a form of active inquiry in which the coach focuses on the positive, on what's working, and on building momentum. It works best when the situation is emotional or the client needs support.

Accountability. Accountability conversations include agreeing on what the client will do between sessions and helping clients move forward when they don't do what they agreed to do.

Shifting the conversation when a client is stuck. A coach can ask questions to help a client get unstuck. The situation dictates which questions to ask.

Role play. Role play is an effective way for the client to hone a crucial conversation, practice a public presentation, or plan to resolve a conflict

Presenting observations with impact. Certain conversations help the coach present observations without coming across as too coercive or pushy.

Letting the client guide the process. When the client and coach have a number of potential directions they can go, the coach uses this type of conversation to let the client guide the process.

The following chapters cover these conversations in more depth. Also, at the end, a chapter gives you guidance about conversations that can help you when you feel stuck during the coaching session.

Agreeing on the Problem and Setting Goals

While we discussed problem definition as part of the coaching process, conversations to agree on the problem and define goals deserve additional clarification. Coaching begins with a problem the client wants to solve or an opportunity the client wants to achieve. Both lead to a goal.

Without a clear problem statement and goal, the coaching will meander. A problem defines a point A and a better point B, with a deadline. For instance:

- I need to increase profits in my unit from $1 million to $1.5 million by the end of the year.

- We need to reduce voluntary turnover by our top talent from 15% to 5% per year by December 31.

- I want to be promoted from branch manager to district manager within the next two years.

Sometimes the coach has to ask questions to help the client set a specific goal. For example, suppose the client states a goal as, "I want Joe to be more engaged in my project." The term "engaged" is pretty vague. If I were coaching this client, I would want to know more about what it would look like if Joe were engaged in the project. If the client went to Joe and said, "Joe, I need you to be more engaged," Joe might reply, "What do you mean? I am engaged." With more questioning from the coach, the client might clarify that Joe should attend three team meetings per week, participate at each meeting, and also speak positively about the project. Now we have something to work with.

A good coaching question to clarify the goal is, "Tell me more about what it would look like if you did achieve this goal?" The reason for defining the problem and setting goals is to be specific enough that there is no doubt about whether or not the goal is achieved. The client will receive value, and the coach knows the session or engagement delivered results.

Sometimes it is hard to define a problem as precisely as the coach might want. Some clients resist getting specific. Some situations are murky. Sometimes the client simply wants to talk things out with an objective listener. All you can do when it comes to goal setting is try your best. At some point, you might feel that you are beating the proverbial dead horse, and the client will want you to move on.

If you let the conversation move forward with an unclear goal, don't be surprised when the session doesn't seem to go anywhere. To paraphrase the Cheshire Cat, if you don't know where you are going, then any direction will get you there. Once the goal is as clear as possible, the coach can keep the conversation on track, for example, asking the client for guidance whenever it seems the conversation is rambling or when the client seems to be discussing a different topic. For instance:

- "I want to check back with you about the initial intent of the session. You mentioned you wanted to achieve X during our meeting. It seems like we are now talking about Y. Let me know if this is okay with you or whether Y connects back to your initial intent."

- "How are we doing in terms of achieving the goal you said you wanted to achieve at the start of the session?"

- "I know you said you wanted to achieve X at the start of the session, but you seem to be talking much more about Y. What would you like to do at this point in the conversation?"

Listening

In almost any form of communication, listening gives you the keys to the kingdom. This fact is even truer in coaching. The coach should be listening 75 percent of the time in a coaching session. Otherwise, you are teaching, mentoring, preaching, directing, or training. Given how much time the coach spends listening, it makes sense to listen with purpose.

First, if you listen well, the client tells you the next question to ask. Once you are present and really hear what the client is saying—both the logical and emotional content as well as what the client isn't saying—coaching becomes easy. The client tells you where to go next! You do much less but get much more. For instance, suppose a client indicates frustration with a conflict. What question is the client telling you to ask?

Many questions can be asked at this point: How would the client like the conflict to be resolved? What is the best approach to resolve the conflict? What does the client know about the other person's style? Where is the common ground? Where is the client willing to be flexible? Where is the client not willing to give ground? What motivates the other person in the situation?

All these questions can be beneficial but they jump ahead a bit and make some assumptions about what the client knows and doesn't know and where the client wants to go. All the client has shared so far is that they have a conflict and are frustrated. What if you added nothing to the conversation beyond what the client has told you? Why not ask, "What would you like to discuss here to get the most out of our time?" It's a simple, high-level question. It assumes nothing and provides the coach with the maximum opportunity to learn from the client and go from there. It also gives the client the opportunity to share what they want to do next. By the way, suppose you can't figure out what to ask the client next. Something you can do—maybe once or twice per coaching session at most—is ask, "If you were the coach, what question would you want me to ask right now?" It works!

Listening comes in many forms, both productive and unproductive. If you have ever taken a $99 hotel seminar about active listening, you know that distracted listening is not helpful. When coaching a client, especially by phone or computer where you can't be seen easily, be sure you are focused. Be present. No matter how much you are tempted, don't multitask, for instance, by typing an email or checking your smart phone for messages while you and the client are talking.

The $99 seminar also teaches you to listen just to listen without fixing, judging, or interrupting to offer your opinion. A slightly more expensive listening seminar might show you how to listen for nonverbal cues and emotions. From there, listening as a coach gets interesting. You can listen by:

- paraphrasing what the client is telling you to be sure that you heard correctly

- reflecting back the emotions you notice to be sure you are empathizing with how the client feels

- understanding the client's interests, commitments, aspirations, and point of view

- drawing a mental map about how the client structures their thinking about an issue

- identifying where the client might be stuck

- observing for how well the client's aspirations and work effort match up

- noticing how coachable the client is
- discover the client's top priorities and values
- identifying the client's communication style
- finding out how aware the client is or isn't about how others are affected
- hearing what the client is not saying
- uncovering the perspectives the client is considering and those the client isn't
- seeing blind spots the client might have in their perceptions or thinking
- identifying limiting perceptions about the issue
- acknowledging the talents and strengths the client has
- finding ways to appreciate the client for their work so far
- noting what gets the client excited and passionate
- determining where the client seems to want to go with the coaching conversation

There are many other ways to listen with purpose. The art of coaching is largely about developing the capacity to listen, which is one of the reasons why developing a culture of coaching in an organization helps leaders, managers, and up-and-coming talent be more effective. By learning to really listen intently, employees learn how to be more collaborative, have more impact, and work more effectively together.

Appreciative Inquiry

Appreciative inquiry is as much a style for a coach as it is a subset of active inquiry. Appreciative inquiry is the same as active inquiry except that the coach emphasizes the positive. Some coaches have a purely appreciative style. Others use appreciative inquiry in situations when the client feels especially vulnerable, is not especially open to criticism, responds best to praise and the positive, or seems to have thin skin.

Appreciative questions are questions that help the client identify how to do better, build on what's working, find support, use their strengths, and consider positive possibilities:

- What's working that you can build on?

- What strengths can you bring to bear on this issue?

- What's a small step you can take to get some traction?

- Who supports you?

- Who can you go to for resources or support?

- What has worked in other areas of your life that you can apply here?

- You mentioned a successful project you did last year. How can you take the lessons from that and apply them to this challenge?

- What becomes possible when you succeed?

- How can you make this initiative the most remarkable of your career?

- How can you make this coming quarter the best financial quarter in the company's history?

Accountability

There are two types of coaching conversations for accountability: the easy one and the hard one. This kind of coaching is a lot like comedian Jerry Seinfeld's observations about rental car companies. According to him, it is easy to take a reservation and hard to keep a reservation. This first accountability coaching conversation is akin to taking a reservation for a rental car. The second is more like keeping the reservation.

The easy conversation—the equivalent of taking a reservation for a car rental—happens when the client gets clarity, and it is time to take action. Your job as a coach is to ask the client what they will do next. Get as specific as possible so that there is no doubt about whether or not the client did what they said they would do. Even here sometimes you have to add a little bit of edge to your coaching and challenge a client who might be thinking too small or holding back. For instance, I recently worked with a client who wanted his branch to be the first one in the nation to implement a new organizational initiative. When I asked him what specifically he would do to make this happen, his plan was vague. He needed some tough coaching to commit to an ambitious, specific goal and a plan to achieve it.

The harder conversation—the equivalent of keeping the car rental reservation—happens when clients don't do what they said they would do. When this happens, it can be challenging to decide how forceful to be. Consider what happens when someone declares a New Year's Resolution to eat less and work out more and then seems to give up. Why does this happen? It isn't rocket science to control portion size, eat fewer snacks, count calories, and navigate to the gym. Something else must be going on beneath the surface. The same is usually true when a client doesn't do what the two of you agreed on. Possibilities might include the following:

- The client isn't really serious about achieving the goal.

- The client isn't accurately calibrating how much work it will take to achieve the goal.

- The client doesn't want to do the work required to be successful.

- The client doesn't have the skills or knowledge to take the action they said they would take.

- The client has time management issues.

- Something else came up that was a bigger priority and might even shift the focus of the coaching.

- The client has limiting beliefs or fear that prevents action.

Given all the unknowns, it makes logical sense to start off by being gentle. Use active inquiry to find out what happened and what the client's considerations were for not taking action. Then discuss those considerations and ask the client to recommit. The coaching could include anything from talking about and working through the client's challenges to role playing, identifying small steps to take instead of large steps, choosing a less ambitious goal, coaching to manage time better, or coaching to shift limiting beliefs. The most effective way to coach a client who isn't taking action is by asking the client for their suggestions. For instance, "How can I best support you so that you do what you committed to do, assuming this is still your intent?"

If the client continues to avoid accountability, perhaps for weeks, then it might be effective to add more edge to your approach. For instance:

- "It's a been a few weeks now, and you've not followed through on your agreement three times in a row. How important is this goal to you?"

- "The current action plan doesn't seem to be working for you. What's plan B?"

- "What's really going on here?"

- "It feels like I care more about getting this done than you. How can I best support you at this point?"

Holding a client accountable is not about judging, blaming, yelling, telling the client what to do, doing the work for the client, or getting impatient. It is about working with the client to find out why the client won't take action and either resolving those challenges or changing the original goal.

Shifting the Conversations
When the Client is Stuck

All coaching is supposed to help the client get unstuck or move ahead more quickly than they are now. Later in this book you will see examples of methodologies that help get people unstuck in specific situations they face. They range from helping clients change their perceptions to addressing specific issues, such as a conflict, engaging employees, or juggling multiple priorities. At the same time, certain conversations can be helpful in general when your client seems stuck.

First, you can ask the client to look at the issue not as a client but as someone giving advice:

- "If you were in my shoes, what would you want me to ask you right now?"

- "Let's say a friend or colleague were in your situation. What advice would you give him or her right now?"

Second, sometimes clients get stuck somewhere on the way to results, which don't just happen. To get a result, someone first has to have a vision about what's possible, develop ideas to make the vision a reality, evaluate and choose from among many ideas, take action, follow up in the face of challenges, and move on to the next goal after getting results. Along the way, there are many places where a client can turn from optimistic to negative or even cynical. Shown on the next page are some coaching questions to help clients along the way.

When the client falls into negativity, complaint, the status quo, frustration, or cynicism, take them back to their vision. With an inspiring and large enough vision, immediate challenges tend to seem small. It is easy to do: "I hear that you are upset. That's actually a good thing because when people are upset it shows that they care. Let's go back to your initial vision. Tell me about what got you so excited about this initiative in the first place."

Sometimes your client gets stuck in the past. Perhaps that person believes that because something failed before it will fail again. Perhaps they resent somebody involved in the new initiative due to some past conflict or offense. If vision doesn't get them back on track, you might have to challenge them to be willing to stop holding onto the past. Either they have to make amends, forgive, or choose to go in a different way from before.

When clients are having conversations about vision, sometimes they will get stuck. These types of clients are often visionaries by nature. They are the dreamers. They are great at talking about an exciting future and can even get others aligned and engaged, but by never leaving the conversation about vision, their colleagues eventually get frustrated. They wonder, "What are next steps? How do we take action?"

To get a client unstuck when they can't seem to get out of the vision conversation, ask, "What are specific ideas to realize your vision?" This will shift most people to brainstorming ideas. Some people love to do this and will never stop unless someone helps them along. They are natural idea generators. The coach can ask, "How do you go about prioritizing these ideas?"

Now the client has to evaluate various ideas. This requires data and analysis. Just as some people are natural visionaries or idea generators, some are natural analysts. These individuals can fall into the trap of analysis paralysis. The coach can help them by saying, "Given that there is never perfect information, if you had to make a choice now, what would it be?" Or, "If you need to do one more round of analysis, how can you make sure that it is the final round before you make a decision?" Once a decision is made, some managers and executives agree on what has to be done, but nobody raises their hand to take action or develop a formal plan. The coach can ask, "What happens next?"

Next, some leaders, managers, and entire teams take some action but quickly get frustrated when things don't move as quickly as they would like. They fall back into negativity and frustration. The coach can take them back to the vision to get them motivated again and also ask them to come up with a contingency plan. At the other end of the spectrum, clients can get so stuck in tasks that they forget about the larger vision and goals. The coach can help them align their work with the actual results they want to achieve.

Finally, once results happen, some clients get stuck here. Rather than acknowledge their success and move on, they bask in the glory of the last successful initiative. They resist moving on to the next idea that will help realize their vision or to a new vision for what's possible beyond what has been achieved. They are like Dorothy and her friends when they fall asleep in the poppy fields near the Emerald City. Now the coach can ask, "What can you do now to keep the vision moving forward? What's the next opportunity or idea to pursue?" These types of shifting questions are quite powerful. Many leaders and executives are skilled at having a certain type of conversation, such as visioning, brainstorming, or developing action plans. The coach looks for opportunities to keep making progress.

Role Play

Role playing with clients can make a significant difference in their effectiveness. When a client has a high-stakes conversation, role playing and rehearsing almost always helps the client have insights about how to be even better during the real event because you and the client have a chance to observe what is already working and areas that need improvement. You also have the opportunity to test out different strategies and learn which approaches work best. When you role play a high-stakes conversation with the client, here are a few suggestions:

- Be very clear about the goal of the client's conversation or presentation. Make sure it is specific. Otherwise, you won't know whether or not the client is achieving their goal.

- Videotape or record the client. Recording gives clients the opportunity to watch themselves in action and draw conclusions about whether or not they really have the impact they intend to have.

- Ask the client for advice about how you should play the role of the other person. What is your style? What objections should you raise? Play with scenarios in which you are more or less difficult in the role of the other person.

- Before jumping into formal role play, let the client vent for a couple of minutes. This is a way for the client to get out everything they can't say in polite company but really would like to say. Let the client swear, insult the other party, and say things as harshly as they want. Sometimes what the client says during this venting time turns out to be the best approach; some clients hold back and don't say what needs to be said.

- How the client opens the conversation is what usually needs the most work. Clients tend to ramble, give too many reasons, or go in a different direction from their stated goal. Give the client about two minutes to open. Then stop and review. Spend enough time on the opening so that the client starts off efficiently and effectively.

- Let the client go first when it is time to discuss how they did during the role play. Don't behave like the stereotypical acting coach who barks out instructions. As with all coaching, after a bit of role play, ask the client what they think worked and what could have been better. Then get back into the role play. From time to time, if it seems the client is missing something major, ask permission to make a suggestion and then share your idea. Less is more.

- Experiment with different approaches. Most people have a natural communication style, which isn't always the right one to use in a specific situation. Role play allows you and the client to try a variety of styles and approaches. The phrase "role play" has the word "play" in it. Treat the experience like a playground. Have fun. Keep it loose. That will help the client relax and keep improving.

Presenting Observations with Impact

The coach enables the client to have insights and move forward. His primary tools are powerful questions and insightful listening. Some coaching purists take these facts a bit too far. They believe coaches should never provide advice or their own observations. This philosophy makes no sense, especially if you have expertise and knowledge and the client values your input. Why wouldn't you share observations and insights that can help the client improve?

Unfortunately, as noted throughout this book, leaders, managers, and high-potential talent are not always open to hearing advice. They have to be coachable, and clients can go in and out of being coachable more frequently than we wish. Therefore, if you have observations to offer your client, you have to present them in a way the client is willing to hear. Following is a suggested approach to do this:

- First, let the client explore issues on their own through the powerful questions that active inquiry requires. Remember the metaphor of the steam vent. Your clients need to vent and let out some figurative steam—to create space before they are open to your advice.

- When the client seems to have exhausted an issue and you still believe you have something valuable to offer, ask permission. For instance, "Do you mind if I offer an observation?"

- If the client says yes, then offer your observation, insight, or advice.

- Let the client respond. I have observed coaches who will give their advice, leave it hanging, and then say, "Okay, time is up. See you next time." Don't do this. Give your advice the respect it deserves. Ask the client for their thoughts about it.

- Don't take it personally if the client doesn't accept your suggestion. Avoid getting into an argument or a debate. Your clients don't have the same experience, style, or attitudes as you do. Ultimately, the client has to be accountable for getting results and will do so their way and at their pace. If you want the client to do it your way, you are no longer a coach. You are either a manager, a consultant, an advisor, or a teacher.

- Help the client get clarity about how they will integrate their own insights with your advice. What happens next? What will the client do and by when?

Letting the Client Guide the Process

It takes a specific type of conversation to let the client guide the coaching process. Avoid stepping in right away and directing the coaching conversation with your own lines of logic or checklists.

At the very beginning of a session, ask clients what they want to achieve. Then before asking for a data dump about the situation ask what the client's ideas are to get there. If you reach a fork in the road, let the client choose which direction to go. For instance, suppose the client tells you three reasons they have for being unproductive. Avoid saying, "I really like that first reason. Let's start there." Instead, let the client guide the process by asking, "Which of the three would you like to discuss first?"

Similarly, it is common for a client to start a coaching session with one goal in mind and then identify new challenges and goals. The client might gain more value by discussing the new issue rather than the original one. The only way to know for sure is by asking the client. For instance, "We started the session with the goal of resolving a conflict you are having, but now you are talking about the overall culture of your team. Which would you like to discuss in the time we have left?" At the end of the session, ask the client what value they got from the session and what they will do next. Ask what they want to discuss next time.

The client will tell you about the coaching they want. The most effective coaches realize this and do less rather than more. They let clients tell them which way the conversation should go. They don't need to be the smartest person or the hero saving the day. Coaching is about working with already effective people. Give your clients the respect they deserve, and let them guide the process.

When You Are Stuck

At some point as a coach, you will get stuck. Coaching is hard, and not all clients are as aware and coachable as we might like. It is the coach's job to determine what to do when they feel stuck. Here are some common situations:

The client asks you for ideas right away.

When the client asks for your ideas to solve their problem, this is a trap to avoid. If you give the client your answers before taking time to understand the client's situation, you are likely to give advice that might work for you but won't work for the client's experience, skill, style, and perceptions. You set yourself up for the client to resist your ideas and get into a debate.

Instead, tell the client that you have some ideas (assuming that you do) but want to understand their thinking first. After all, you both have different styles, and what's right for you might not be right for the client. If you can't help yourself or the client insists on hearing your ideas, let the client know they probably won't like them, because—again—you are not the same person. If the client doesn't like what you have to say, this gives you the opportunity to reply, "I told you that you wouldn't like my ideas. Now it's your turn. What would you do in this situation?"

The client still has no idea what to do.

If the client seems stuck, some questions that can help include the following listed on the next page:

- "What advice would you give to a colleague with the same problem?"
- "What skills do you have that apply here?"
- "Who can you go to for advice?"
- "Who has handled this situation really well in the past? What did they do?"
- "What are situations outside of work that you handled that are similar to this? What worked that you might apply here?"
- "If you could do anything at all with no fear or repercussions and money and time were no object, what would you do?"

One question that will seem completely ridiculous but works much of the time is: "If you did know the answer, what would it be?" This question somehow gets beyond logical thinking and encourages the client to be creative. I can't explain why, but it works a good percentage of the time.

You run out of questions to ask the client.

What if you draw a blank and run out of things to ask the client? Here are three options:

First, ask the client what they would ask if they were the coach. This is a great way to learn about the client's thought process in the moment.

Second, take a moment to summarize what you have heard and confirm you and the client are on the same page. Then ask the client where they want to go from here.

Third, ask the client what, if any, insights they have had up to this point. This might open up new areas to discuss.

The client rambles, and this frustrates you.

Some clients seem to ramble on and on. If you have a client who does this and it frustrates you, it will be hard for you to focus on what they are saying. You might feel that you are three steps ahead of the client and already know the answer.

The best approach in this situation is patience. Some clients will have different ways of communicating from how you communicate. They could be more process oriented and need to go into the details. Also, they might appreciate taking time to think things through out loud with you. Recognize that you are providing value to the client by letting them process their issues. Don't worry about whether or not you are getting to talk enough. Don't fret if you can't always be the superhero who saves the day with your fast, brilliant insights. Be patient and wait for your opportunity to share your observations or challenge the client to think bigger if appropriate.

Another approach is to ask the client about how the coaching is going. For instance, "I want to be sure you are getting value from our sessions. I notice that you are doing most of the talking, and I'm not sure if that is working for you or not. Please let me know." If the client is all over the place, ask them where they want to focus. For example: "I hear you talking about three things: X, Y, and Z. Which of these is most important to discuss now?" Or, "When we first started, you said you wanted to talk about X. Now you are talking about Y. Help me understand how they are connected or which one you want to focus on now?" Of course, if the client is working specifically with you to be more concise, then you do have an opportunity to challenge the client to express their thoughts more efficiently.

The client doesn't keep their agreements.

Coaching clients are typically busy people with many priorities. Sometimes they have to cancel sessions. Sometimes they come late. Sometimes they don't do what they said they would do. Keeping the busy schedules of most coaching clients in mind, I suggest that you start out gently. Ask what happened and what you and the client can do to prevent that from happening in the future.

If the client continues to break their agreements, this can be a sign that they also break agreements outside the coaching session. A 360-degree verbal assessment can confirm if this is true. If it is, then focusing on these behaviors can lead to insights about the client's habits and perceptions and help them be more effective. At some point, you can change your style to have a bit more edge. For instance, "You are late for the fourth time in four sessions. Is our coaching relationship important to you?"

The client is emotional.

Sometimes clients get emotional. That's a sign of powerful coaching, although it is not required, and you shouldn't feel that you need your client to experience a major catharsis when you coach them. If the client gets emotional, roll with it. Give the client the time they need to process their emotion. Ask what they would like to do.

Sometimes the client will want to keep moving ahead. Sometimes the client needs a few minutes to calm down. And sometimes the client will be so distracted that rescheduling the session is best.

You already are 100 percent sure that know the answer, and you don't need to ask more questions.

We have covered this issue before, but it is so important that it is worth repeating. Again, wherever possible, coaches are most effective when they let the client work things out. However, let's assume that the client has an issue that is right smack in the middle of your sweet spot of expertise. For instance, they might be wrestling with an operational issue, and you happen to be an expert on operations in the client's industry and even company. If you know the answer so certainly that you can't focus on coaching the client anymore, simply call a time out and say, "I hope you don't mind, but I feel like I need to break out of my coaching role for a moment. I happen to be an expert in this area. Do you mind if I put on a consulting or advisory hat for a bit?"

The client has other distractions that are more urgent than the current coaching.

Ask what the client wants to do. Some clients will want to talk through the urgent issues and need to do so before they can focus on the stated intent of the coaching. At other times, clients might need to reschedule the session to a better time. Again, let the client guide the process.

If a pattern of having constant fires continues, you might ask the client if they want to discuss it in more depth. Constantly fighting fires and having urgent issues come up prevents effective strategic focus and often leads to burnout. It also can serve as a way for the client to avoid having conversations about the main goal of the coaching.

Part Four

COACHING SITUATIONS: INDIVIDUAL EFFECTIVENESS

Overview

Each chapter in this section covers a different issue that leaders, managers, and up-and-coming talent face and that improve individual effectiveness. The next sections raise issues related to building strong relationships and using coaching to move organizational initiatives forward. The topics covered in this section include:

- Get grounded: Who does the client need to be as a leader?
- Coach to change or develop a new behavior
- Coach to shift a limiting perception
- Communicate simply and powerfully
- Influence others
- Manage time and overcome overwhelm
- Think comprehensively about an issue
- Develop leadership presence

Get Grounded: Who Does The Client Need To Be As A Leader?

If you are coaching a leader, executive, manager, and up-and-coming talent to be a better leader, a great place to start is by helping the client get grounded about who they need to be as a leader. The client answers a series of simple but profound, important question to clarify who they are and what they stand for. Before you coach somebody else on this topic, please answer these questions about your own role as a leader. The questions are:

- "What is your vision for your area of responsibility?" Help clients define where they are taking their organization in the future.

- "What is your vision for your career?" Coach clients on their vision for what they can make happen in their career.

- "What are your core values as a leader?" Values are fundamental attributes about how the leader shows up.

- "What do you stand for as a leader?" Leaders stand for more than making money or surviving the next layoff.

- "What is your purpose?" In other words, what contribution do you want to make, and why?

- "What is your unique edge as a leader?" Coach the leader to clarify what sets them apart from others. The answer could include talents, strengths, skills, knowledge, relationships, and past experiences upon which to build.

- "What are your top priorities as a leader?" Answering this question helps the leader to focus their time.

- "What are the metrics that measure your success?" While vision, mission, and values are crucial, they mean nothing if the leader fails to achieve results.

- "What are the key behaviors and attitudes that you will model?" Leaders send messages with every decision they make and action they take. By determining key habits to model, leader can send consistent messages and show others what they really stand for.

- "Who are your key relationships?" Leaders engage, mobilize, and work effectively with other people to get results. They nurture professional relationships while also   continuing to improve.

- "What is your plan to continue to develop professionally and personally?" Leaders never stop growing.

The above questions are not easy to answer. One approach is to give these questions to your clients to contemplate on their own time before meeting with you. Ask clients to write down their answers to each question in a concise document. Then have a coaching session to follow up. Ask the client about which questions they would like to discuss and help them develop clarity. After the coaching session, the client can refine the answers to these questions in more depth. The outcome of this work is that clients have a living, breathing document about their most important priorities and what they stand for as a leader. The two of you can bring it out from time to time to discuss it, update it, and handle any current challenges. Meanwhile, clients have a short document that helps them stay grounded and focused as a leader.

Coach to Change or Develop a New Behavior

One of the simplest and most powerful forms of coaching is behavioral coaching. In a behavioral coaching process, the coach works with the client to discover and change one behavior that will have the biggest impact on their performance. Behavioral coaching can be valuable in a number of situations:

- As part of general leadership coaching, the client wants to find the one behavior that will make the biggest difference in their performance. Baseball offers a useful metaphor for this situation. A baseball player who gets eight hits out of thirty at bats has a batting average of .267, which is considered to be mediocre. If that player can get just one more hit in every thirty at bats—only one more hit—his average goes up to .300, which can make him millions in additional salary. And yet, one more hit out of thirty is an increase of only 3.3%. If he can make even one more hit out of thirty, he has a .333 batting average, which can make him an All-Star. What we are looking for today is that one behavior for you that will be the equivalent of getting one or two more hits at work. We are looking for you to choose one behavioral change that might seem minor but can lead to major improvements in results.

- The client has a behavioral blind spot that is holding back or even derailing their career. For instance, they exhibit a pattern of behaviors that show up as arrogance. Alternatively, perhaps they avoid conflict in ways that hurt productivity.

- The client has a limiting belief, perception, or attitude that is holding them back. Behaviors are expressions of our beliefs, perceptions, and attitudes. By combining perceptual coaching with behavioral coaching, the client can provide tangible evidence that the new ways of thinking are taking root.

- The client is trying to change the habits of the entire organization and first needs to model those same behaviors. Leaders go first.

Behavioral coaching has the advantage of being measurable. The client either makes the new behavior a habit or doesn't. We can observe and monitor results. There is nowhere to hide. The approach has two parts.

First, choose a behavior. The client chooses a simple, specific, and measurable behavior to start doing, stop doing, do more, or do less. The key is that this behavior is simple, specific, measurable, and stated in a positive way. Examples include letting people finish speaking, smiling more, praising the team more often, criticizing privately instead of in team meetings, making eye contact, giving employees informal feedback once each week, and confirming understanding after giving instructions

Avoid subjective patterns, judgments, and conclusions. For instance, arrogance is a subjective conclusion that we make about someone after observing a variety of behaviors that come together. Specific behaviors under the umbrella of arrogance might include interrupting, making dismissive comments, rolling eyes, folding arms, sighing loudly when others speak, raising one's voice, and making personal attacks. Different people express arrogance in different ways.

Subjective themes, such as arrogance, should be avoided because coaching works better when choosing one simple behavior rather than a whole pattern. People don't respond well to subjective labels. If you were told that you were arrogant, sloppy, passive-aggressive, abrasive, difficult, stubborn, or that you lacked integrity, how would you respond? In contrast, if you were challenged to let people finish speaking without interrupting, you would probably be more accepting. Also, behaviors that fit a pattern, such as arrogance, usually go together. If you choose one behavior to work on with a client, they will also need to discuss the others. In other words, by choosing a specific behavior, the coach and client handle the overall pattern regardless.

A final reason to choose a simple and specific behavior is that the behavioral coaching process includes getting feedback and advice from colleagues. During this process, colleagues comment on both the specific behavior in question as well as other things they notice. The client should ultimately choose the behavior. If you did a proper assessment, you and the client will have plenty of data from colleagues, performance reviews, an off-the-shelf assessment, the client's own observations, and what the sponsor of the coaching has to say.

Once you choose the behavior, the second step is to make the new behavior a habit. It takes time and support to create a new habit, especially for already successful professionals. The process requires the coach and client to work together for anywhere between six months and a year before the new behavior fully takes root. Of course, during this process, there is plenty of time for coaching on other issues to help the client keep getting better. Shown below is a step-by-step process based on cognitive psychology to coach a client to make a new behavior a habit.

First, take notes. To start the process, ask the client to take notes about incidences that happen while they try to make the new behavior a habit—both positive and negative. What happened? When? What was the trigger? What worked? What did they learn? What will they try next time? By taking notes, you and the client have data about what's really happening. You can look for patterns and also coach the client to tackle each challenge one at a time. As the coaching progresses, the client should see the notes emphasize more and more positive results.

Second, build in a monthly 360-degreee feedback process. This process takes courage, but it works beautifully. It is very loosely based on a process that pioneering coach Marshall Goldsmith showed me when I had the chance to shadow him almost two decades ago. (For more information about the way Marshall Goldsmith currently teaches this process, read his book *What Got You Here Won't Get You There*).

To begin the feedback process, coach and client choose around five allies who will offer monthly feedback. Their time commitment is not more than twenty minutes per month. Every month the client asks each person, in person or by phone (not email!), how often they observed the new behavior, overall advice about what the client has been doing well and, if applicable, one thing that the client could be doing better. Each person rates how often they observed the new behavior used productively, using a scale of one to five.

The client's job is to receive the feedback professionally, avoid getting defensive, ask questions to direct the feedback in a useful way, and thank each person for the advice. You might have to role play with the client and coach them to get better at receiving feedback with grace. The client's goal is to go three consecutive months getting an average score of at least a four or a five in terms of how often their colleagues see the new behavior. This is a great way to create an open, transparent culture where people trust each other enough to give and receive advice. After all, how many teams and organizations do you know where leaders give and receive feedback and advice as naturally as they cash their paychecks? It also ensures that the coaching process includes a way to measure and track results and know when the client has achieved the goal.

Third, work with the client to stay on track while they still take notes and get feedback. A number of proven ways can be used to support and reinforce a new habit. If your client experiences challenges staying on track and you believe that additional support is needed beyond the coaching, use any of the following techniques. Add no more than one per coaching session or you risk overwhelming the client.

Preplanning

Before an event that is likely to challenge the client, you can help them preplan what they will and won't do in the meeting. Athletes do the same thing before going into a big game. They visualize different scenarios and how they will react when those happen during the game.

Self-talk

When the client feels the temptation to go back to old ways, it helps to talk to themselves about what they will and won't do and also the consequences that are likely to follow. Self-talk can be both positive and negative. Positive self-talk convinces the client about what they will do and the good things that will result. For instance, "Joe is driving me nuts in this meeting, but I am going to relax and let him finish. If I do, then he will feel more engaged and is more likely to do what he needs to do. Also, my career will move ahead."

Negative self-talk emphasizes the consequences. For instance, "If I don't smile when I am happy, people will get mixed messages about how I really feel and also think I am angry. I'll be known as the office sad sack, and my career will never go anywhere." Talking out loud to oneself works best, although for obvious reasons this is not a good tactic to use in public setting.

Rewards

We don't like to think of ourselves like Pavlov's dogs, but rewards do reinforce desired behaviors. Rewards are often built into the process. When client use more effective behaviors, they get better response, have more impact, and get better results. Sometimes, however, the client can also choose additional rewards.

Role play

Role play helps the client get comfortable with new behaviors that involve interacting with others.

Practice, drills, and repetitive training

These activities can ingrain new behaviors. They work well with individuals and teams. For instance, many health systems run drills in anticipation of a major disaster or health crisis. Similarly, you can test individuals with different scenarios that might challenge them in everyday situations.

Stress reduction

When we are stressed, we are more likely to fall back into automatic ways of doing things. Stress reduction can take many forms that can work for clients. Please be careful about evangelizing about your own favorite form of stress reduction. Just because you love hot yoga or meditation doesn't mean that the client will respond the same way. Stress can be relieved in many simple ways: scheduling time to work out, walking around the office campus, changing one's diet, getting a good night's sleep, leaving for work a bit earlier to avoid traffic jams and being late for the first meeting, improving time management skills, and taking a few deep breaths when upset or angry.

Support network

Ask clients who else can support them in making the desired change. For instance, a trusted colleague might be able to send signals during a meeting to remind the client to avoid old behaviors and focus on new ones. He or she can also talk to the client after the meeting about what worked and could have been better.

Self-coaching

At the beginning and end of every day, clients can have a coaching session with themselves about the new behavior. Have them ask themselves questions they would want a coach to ask, share insights that they would want a coach to share with them, and acknowledge what has worked and what they will work on to keep improving.

Conversations that set boundaries

If clients discover that their old patterns of behavior are triggered by others' actions—especially actions that step over the line and infringe on their boundaries—they might need to assert appropriately. For instance, if someone consistently misses deadlines and this causes great stress for your client, it might be time for your client to have a conversation that influences this person to change his or her ways.

Anchoring to negative and positive emotions

By anchoring old behaviors to negative emotions and new behaviors to positive emotions, old habits are more easily broken, and new habits are more easily formed. This technique comes from Neuro Linguistic Programming.

For instance, remembering the poor performance review about the behavior that led to coaching is an example of anchoring to negative emotions. Similarly, some people use elastic bands on their wrist as reminders; they tweak themselves with the band when they are tempted to go back to the old behavior.

On the positive side, clients can imagine how their career will progress after achieving the goal and how they will feel. These positive feelings can help them stay on track. Another way to use the elastic band, or a bracelet, is to put it on the left wrist after doing the desired behavior and on the right wrist after making a mistake.

Vision

Having your clients create a vision statement—and even draw it and post it in their work area—is a great way to keep a goal in mind and stay on track. The client can map out what becomes possible once they make the current behavior a habit. They can refer to their vision as constant encouragement to stay on track. This approach is closely related to anchoring to positive emotions.

Lessons from past successes

Ask clients about when they made a change in the past and what they did to stay on track. Perhaps they lost weight, got in shape, stopped smoking, or applied a new skill at work. Use that success to identify strategies that work best for your client.

As you can see, behavioral coaching is a straightforward, simple process that can have a major impact.

Coach to Shift a Limiting Perception

In one sense, all coaching is perceptual. You and the client discover new ways of thinking about a problem and have new insights about how to make progress and come away with new approaches and action steps. Our attitudes and perceptions shape how we see the world. A bunny rabbit could be a cute and cuddly animal, a tasty meal, a pest that eats crops, a disease-carrying vermin, or an important part of the ecosystem—depending on who is looking at it. The same variation in perception is true for us at work, with all sorts of situations, people, and decisions. What is interesting is that each unique viewpoint is correct; none of them are right or wrong. Too many times we let our perceptions get in the way of our progress because of the level of "fact" we place on them.

As a result, sometimes clients have attitudes and beliefs that are so pervasive and have a significant cost on their productivity and relationships that they will benefit from a focus on shifting perceptions. These ways of perceiving might have served the client in the past but now hold them back. In fact, many of these perceptions probably came about as defense mechanisms or ways to cope and started early in the client's childhood. They occur automatically in the blink of an eye, and the client is often not aware they are reacting on autopilot. Such reactions tend to come up especially during times of stress when the client doesn't have the space to make a conscious choice.

In fact, these perceptions are so pervasive that clients often don't even know they have them. Usually, you can't ask a client, "What are your limiting beliefs?" and expect a good answer. Rather, you will uncover these beliefs after working with a client for some time. You will find them in recurring things that the client says and does—explanations for why things happen the way they do, all or nothing judgments about people or situations, and subjective statements about how the world seems to them.

Coaches can help. Note that we are not talking about therapy. If you are working with someone who seems to have a very deep issue, shows signs of mental illness, or talks about hurting themselves or others, refer them to a licensed mental health professional immediately. We are talking about perceptions that show up for the client at work, and that we can help the client deal with in a work situation. We can do this without asking about the client's childhood, parents, or getting into any deep traumas.

The results are phenomenal. Clients have new ways of seeing things, can grow into new roles, and move on with less effort and stress. They have more choices and enjoy a greater sense of freedom. Meanwhile, by dealing with these issues at work, clients often apply their insights to areas outside of work too.

To start, let's define two common types of limiting perceptions: false priorities and limiting beliefs about oneself.

False priorities

Sometimes we set priorities for ourselves ahead of getting results or being successful. A great question to ask your clients when things are not going well and where they seem to have lost track of outcomes is: "Would you rather be _____ or successful?" Common false priorities include the following:

- Look good. Some people would rather look good than get results. Of course, getting results is the best way to look good, but some people shift blame, take credit, and do all they can to look good, even at the expense of results.

- Enjoy prestige. If you would rather have the fancy title, think about who has the best office, compare the things you have to what others have, and are not thinking primarily about results for customers and for your organization, this one might be a false priority.

- Be right. Some managers are all about being right. This is the "I told you so" mentality, which also shows up when a manager wants to win at all costs, including cost to relationships and to the team.

- Get credit. Would you rather get credit or be successful? Some managers don't get results because they care too much about making sure everyone knows they are the ones who came up with the idea or made things happen. As a result, others don't want to play along. Share the credit.

- Be smart. In professional services firms, such as law firms and consulting firms, sometimes people would rather be seen as the smartest person in the room than come up with practical ideas that actually get implemented.

- Be funny. There is a great payoff for being funny, but using humor can also be a strategy to avoid getting results.

- Be interesting or eccentric. Ditto.

- Be liked. Newer managers often struggle with this, especially if they come through the ranks. They don't want to lose their friends, who now report to them, and so they go for popularity over making tough decisions and being respected.

- Have peace and harmony on your team. Many of us avoid conflict at almost any cost. In fact, appropriate conflict is important to having good, open discussions and exploring different angles of a decision. Conflict taken too far is unproductive, however, and managers need to find that right balance between avoiding appropriate conflict and pushing too hard.

- Be perfect. Some of us have the perfection syndrome. We want perfect data. We fall into analysis paralysis. We keep trying to perfect products and ideas instead of testing them and improving as we go. In today's world of Internet marketing, the need for perfection can be a liability.

- Be the hero. Some would rather let the team fail and then jump in and be Superman.

- Get attention.

- Be above it all. This is the aloof manager who won't deal with the masses.

- Dominate, thwart, or sabotage someone else.

- Escape or hide out. Sometimes we avoid issues when the going gets tough instead of facing up to them.

- Avoid being involved. If you tend to throw your hands up when things go wrong, this is a potential issue to discuss.

- Say, "I told you so!" This is the blamer and also a different way of being right instead of getting results.

Limiting beliefs about oneself

The second category of limiting perceptions is beliefs that we hold about our own self and that hold us back. For instance:

- I am not good enough.

- I am not smart enough.

- I can't trust other people.

- I need to be in control.

- I can't make a decision without perfect information.

- I can't let anything leave my office until it is perfect.

- Anytime I fail, it means that I am a failure.

- I am not likeable.

- I think that conflict is bad.

- No one can do it as well as I can.

- I can't find good people.

- I need to be liked.

- This project (or company) is my baby.

- Only I can get this done.

- I need to stay in control.

- Amazing things never happen to me.

- I can't show people my human side.

The approach to handling these perceptions is similar to behavioral coaching because the bulk of the work is about making new habits. In the case of perceptual coaching, you work with the client on new ways of perceiving as well as on new behaviors that reflect the changed view. The tactics that create new habits—note taking, getting support, preplanning, and so on—are the same as what we covered in the last chapter. The only new wrinkle is helping the client come up with new beliefs, perceptions, attitudes, and ways of thinking.

One challenge in doing this is that it is extremely difficult to help someone eliminate a perception or habitual way of thinking that they have held for years. Think of the mind as a vinyl record. Our thoughts are like the grooves in the record. The longer we have held the thought or belief, the deeper the groove. Our core perceptions and beliefs are so deep that they are hard to erase. In fact, if the client were to challenge the belief by saying it isn't true, all they would do is wake up the old belief. For instance, suppose you are working with someone who doesn't trust people. You can debate logically with that person all day long about the fact that some people are trustworthy and some aren't, and it won't make any difference to them. You can challenge the client to repeat, "I can trust people," but that will only cause them to remember all the reasons why they can't trust people.

The only way out of this challenge is to help the client choose an alternative perception and make it a habit. It takes commitment, discipline, and practice, but it is proven to work.

For instance, you can use the "if/then" format as a template to reframe a limiting belief about oneself. Many of our limiting perceptions are blanket statements. What we can do is come up with a narrower, more specific statement of what we can do to get a result. For instance, if we don't trust people in general, we can say, "If I give my employees the training, support, and resources they need, they will get the job done." Notice that the word "trust" doesn't appear here. You don't have to compete with the long-standing belief about not trusting others. What's compelling about this approach is that the client takes a blanket statement and turns it into a statement where they control their situation with simple things that they can do.

For clients with false priorities, you can use the same if/then template. In this case, you build on the client's need for a particular outcome—such as looking good or being liked—with a new path to get there. Suppose a client values being popular, sometimes at the cost of saying what needs to be said and getting results. A reframing might be: "If I assert appropriately about what I expect, people will get better results, their careers will advance, and then they will gravitate toward me."

A second approach is to come up with a mantra, which is a short statement that the client repeats again and again. In the case of not trusting employees, the mantra might be: "Support them. Support them. Support them." If the client needs everything to be perfect before taking action, a mantra might be: "Take small steps. Take small steps."

A third approach to reframe a belief is to choose a creative alternative. For instance, an alternative to the belief "conflict is bad" might be that appropriate assertion is an important tool for any manager. Patrick Lencioni is a master of creative alternatives, for instance, in his book *The Five Temptations of the CEO*. For each of the five temptations he reveals—status, being popular, harmony, invulnerability, and the need for perfect information—he offers a creative alternative: results, being respected, appropriate conflict, trust, and making quick decisions. It is not easy to come up with a creative alternative, and sometimes you and the client can look to business authors and experts for ideas.

A fourth approach is to help the client come up with a metaphor that will help them see things differently. I worked with a client who felt he didn't have anything valuable to offer. When we explored the issue, he shared that his parents owned a farm and eventually sold it to become financially independent. My client, who was a consultant, believed he had nothing valuable to offer because "value" to him meant having something tangible, such as a farm and the products that a farm produces. Eventually, he realized that "My knowledge and expertise are my farm!" The metaphor of a farm allowed him to break through to new ways of thinking.

Examples of reframing:

LIMITING PERCEPTION	REFRAMED
I can't trust other people to get the job done.	If I provide ongoing training, resources, and support and if I follow up, people will do what needs to be done.
Everything must be perfect.	By testing and improving and by taking small steps along the way, we eventually achieve perfection.
I am not smart enough to move up.	If I focus on outcomes and the needs of our customers, rewards will follow.
Conflict is bad.	Appropriate assertion, negotiation, and feedback are powerful tools to achieve my goals.
I need to be loved by everyone.	My family loves me. I want my employees to respect me.

It is not your job as a coach to give the client a bright and shiny reframed belief. You can offer suggestions and ideas, but the client has to embrace and own the new belief. Steps in this process include the following:

- Clients first have to agree that a current perception or belief is no longer serving them. Otherwise, they won't be coachable. You can ask the client permission to share your observation that the client might have a way or perceiving things that isn't working, but only the client can agree and choose to get coaching to reframe their thinking.

- Let the client know that you can't eliminate the current belief or perception. Remember the metaphor of the vinyl record.

- Offer to reframe the perception and then coach the client to make the new way of thinking a habit.

- Show the client different ways to reframe, and give examples like the ones above.

- Ask clients to choose a new way of perceiving that works for them. This can take some time. Give clients the space they need to come up with ideas. You know they have found something when their facial expressions, body language, and tone of voice shift to become more positive and relaxed.

- Ask the client about new behaviors and outcomes that become possible with the new perception. This step is crucial because it allows the new beliefs and attitudes to show up and get results.

- Work with the client to make the new perception and associated behaviors a habit. Use the behavioral coaching process from the previous chapter.

An alternative: creating a new, positive perception from scratch

For some clients, the perceptual issue is not so much about limiting ways of perceiving but rather that they have the opportunity to generate new attitudes and ways of thinking from scratch. It is a great practice to identify positive perceptions, key leadership attitudes, and more productive ways of perceiving the world and work to make those habitual. You don't need any kind of leadership guru to help you with this work. I am sure you and your clients could come up with a lengthy list of key leadership attitudes and perceptions.

If you would like some idea joggers, here are six attitudes that have worked with some of my clients:

One: "Yes, and . . ." This attitude comes from the world of improvisational acting and comedy. "Yes, and . . ." is about accepting what the other person says and building on it. At most organizations, the default attitude is "No, but . . ." Leaders build on ideas, on vision, and on possibility. They welcome new ideas and the contributions of other people. They explore ideas before shooting them down. Even if you are skeptical or don't like the idea at first, the "Yes, and . . ." attitude at least means you work with the other person to understand his or her thinking and see what it could make possible. Imagine meetings where people share their ideas and aren't shot down immediately—where people thank them for the idea, build on the idea, and try the idea on. That is the spirit of "Yes, and . . ."

Two: Vision. Leaders have vision. Vision alone is not enough to get results, and executing on vision can be extraordinarily difficult, but vision is the starting point. Leaders see the big picture. They shift perspective to the future, then back to the present, and then set a course back to the future. They have an inclusive vision beyond their own small and petty wants. When setbacks happen, the leader brings people back to the vision of what's possible so that the setback seems small in comparison. The leader becomes a source of confidence, possibility, and resolve, even when others feel down, are doubtful, or don't want to do the hard work required to succeed.

Three: I care. This is a tough one because we live in cynical times, and we have seen many leaders in the past that care only about themselves and not about their organization, customers, or employees. Authentic leadership is fundamentally about caring, caring about the success of each employee, caring about key strategic initiatives, caring about the organization's success, and caring about the customers and the value they get from the organization's products and services. In other words, the leader is engaged. It is certainly easier to get results, including those that serve one's own aspirations, when your client cares.

Four: I can. I am accountable and responsible. Leaders get things done and have a positive attitude that challenges can be met. If a leader says he or she will do something, it happens, even if the leader doesn't feel like it, even if others are in the way. Most importantly, leaders take responsibility for their impact and results. If I have a meeting with someone and it doesn't go the way I wanted it to, it is not the other person's responsibility. It means I didn't communicate effectively, and I need to regroup and come up with a better approach. If my relationship with my boss is not as strong as it could be, I don't blame my boss. I take responsibility for understanding my boss and improving it. The leader identifies what is working and what isn't and takes steps to build on what's working and address what isn't without drama. It also doesn't mean stepping in and micromanaging or doing all the work but rather taking responsibility for influencing others to do their part too.

Five: Focus on outcomes while finding a proper balance of managing relationships and ego. It is relatively easy to get results, one time, if the leader doesn't care about relationships, but we are in our careers over the long haul. We need to balance relationships, results, and our ego. Starting with ego, the fact is that leaders have healthy egos. At the same time, they also keep their egos in check. They give credit. They accept responsibility. They would rather be successful than right, smart, or the one with the fanciest car. Without keeping our egos in check, we get our priorities wrong. Next, the leader has to get results, but if the leader pushes too hard, that person hurts relationships. They come across as obnoxious, arrogant, or too forceful. This works once, but it kills relationships. Third, the leader has to balance ego and results with relationships. If the leader focuses too much on preserving relationships, that individual avoids tough decisions and doesn't get results. A leader balances all three: ego, results, and relationships.

Six: The success laboratory. Finally, leaders keep learning and getting better. If leaders don't get results, they don't keep doing the same thing over and over, hoping that something changes. They don't have a tantrum or give up. They learn. A poor result is nothing more than data. It doesn't mean anything. We say, "Hmmmm . . ." and develop another approach. We keep learning. Similarly, a good result becomes something we learn from and try again until we know exactly when that approach works and doesn't. Success becomes a science. We build on what works and eliminate what doesn't. We take small risks to keep learning. In marketing, we don't roll out a multimillion dollar campaign without first testing it on a small scale. If it works, we roll it out gradually. If it doesn't, we tweak it and try a small test, or we get rid of the idea and try something else. We don't put our careers on the line with huge bets, but rather we take a measured approach to learn what works. The same is true in almost any discipline at work, and it also applies to leadership. Most people take results much too personally. The attitude of seeing work as a success laboratory deals with this problem.

Again, I'm not suggesting that the above six attitudes are the only ones or the right ones. You as a coach can help clients develop positive attitudes in many ways. I have worked with clients to develop many other attitudes, including resilience, ability to handle ambiguity, persistence, courage, and creativity.

Perhaps your own organization has a set of values or desired attitudes. Still, if you take all six of these attitudes together, you have a leader who makes things happen, sees possibility, has a positive attitude, and keeps learning and getting better—all while building positive relationships. The ultimate goal of perceptual coaching is that the client discovers that they can create their own emotional state based on what will be most effective in a given situation, and that they don't have to be reactive. Perceptual coaching can be incredibly powerful, whether you are reframing current beliefs or helping make new beliefs and attitudes habitual.

Communicate Simply and Powerfully

You can help an executive, manager, business owner, or up-and-coming talent to improve their communication in many ways. This chapter focuses on three areas that come up frequently.

Giving a public presentation

First, you can coach your clients when they have a major public presentation coming up. Public speaking can be a nerve-racking experience. I know a CEO of a Fortune 500 company that was waiting to go onstage to make a presentation to a group of 1,500 people at a conference. Backstage he shared, "What they say is true. Public speaking scares me almost as much as dying a painful death."

You don't need to be a Broadway star or radio personality to help your clients become more comfortable before a major presentation and also help them improve their speaking skills. All you have to do is watch them give the presentation. You can videotape it and perhaps even invite a few trusted colleagues to review it. Ask your client what they think worked and what they want to keep improving. Review the videotape to make sure your client sees how they really come across. Ask any audience members for their advice about what worked and what could be better. Then repeat until the client is more comfortable and has the impact they want to have.

There are dozens of things that clients don't even know they are doing when presenting that are hurting their impact. Examples range from death by PowerPoint to a poor opening; a rambling middle;

a mushy end; issues with voice volume and tone; hand and facial gestures that don't work; using empty words, such as "um"; and pacing back and forth across the stage like a tiger. You can even buy any of the thousands of public speaking books on the market before you coach your client, or Google a list of top public speaking tips to become an instant expert. As always when coaching, please let your client guide the process. Ask what they liked and didn't like, where they might want advice, and what they want to do next to keep refining the presentation.

Communication style flexibility

Second, many leaders and managers suffer because they have only one or two communication styles. An approach you can use to help your client develop greater flexibility is to use parts of the body as a metaphor for different styles of communication. Different situations call for different styles. You and your client can brainstorm together and then role play to discover and practice the best style for a given situation.

Left Brain. The left brain represents facts, logic, data, and reasons. We communicate from the left brain when we want to convince someone that, logically, an idea makes sense. The best way to do that is by finding reasons and facts that matter to the other person. A good format for this is, "I suggest X. Here's why . . ." and then give two but no more than three of the best reasons you can to support your suggestion. If you give more than three reasons, you dilute your argument. For instance, "Joe, I suggest you start coming to the project meetings on time. First, you are losing credibility by coming late, and if you start coming on time the team will regain respect for you. Second, your manager is noticing this behavior, and so not coming on time is not good for your career." In this case, I used negative reasons. I could have also been more positive: "By coming on time, you'll show your manager that you are committed to this project, and you are more likely to advance your career. Also, your team will respect you even more than they already do."

A second approach that uses the left brain is called the rule of three. For some reason, we can't remember many more than three points at a time. We communicate most powerfully when we use this rule. To practice the rule of three with your clients, challenge them to answer the following questions:

- What are up to three talents you have?

- What are up to three things that your organization does better than any other?

- What are three traits you require from prospective hires?

- What are three performance goals you must achieve to be successful?

Finally, you can play a game called "That's exactly why . . ." with your client. This is a great game for using your left brain. Proposing ideas is a start but not enough. Your client is likely to receive objections, and it is important to be able to respond. This game is great practice for doing that. Here is how it works: Your client proposes an idea to you. Then you say, "No," and give a reason. The reason doesn't have to make sense. It just has to be a reason. The client's job is to then say, "That's exactly why my idea makes sense" and tell you why. For instance, suppose you say, "I suggest we go to Chinese food for lunch. You have said you wanted to try something new, and a great new Chinese restaurant has opened right next door. You also said you want to eat healthier, and this restaurant has a low-calorie menu." As the coach, you might reply, "No. I've never liked Chinese food." You could give any reason, from "Chinese food makes me queasy" to "I don't like the color of your shirt today and don't want to be seen in public with you."

Challenge your client to come up with a good response to whatever you say. For instance, suppose you have told the client, "I just don't like

Chinese food." Decide what would be a good response that begins with "That's exactly why you should come with me today." One example might be "That's exactly why you should come with me today. Flexibility is the sign of a great leader, and coming with me for Chinese food will be a great way to develop more flexibility." Another might be "That's exactly why you should come with me today. I don't like hamburgers, but you dragged me to that hamburger joint last week. Today, it is only fair that I get to take you to a place you think you won't like." Another might be "No worries. This place has a great salad buffet and other non-Chinese dishes, and the kitchen staff is very responsive to your custom requests."

The reasons don't have to be great. The key is that your client is willing to try. You are helping your client build the muscle of responding to objections using facts and logic. Make sure the facts matter as much as possible to the other person.

Right brain. The right brain is where we paint pictures with words, use metaphors, and tell stories that help people see your point of view and that can even move them emotionally. Human beings used to sit around fires telling stories because stories connect powerfully with people. As leaders, each of us should have an arsenal of stories that we tell: stories about how we overcame challenges to achieve a success; stories about what our mentors taught us; stories about our favorite characters from the movies, literature, and history and how their lives apply to current challenges. We don't want to overdo it and be seen as a blowhard, but we do want to mix it up by using stories from time to time. Your clients should be able to do the same.

If you have clients that could benefit from a bit more of the right brain in their communications, challenge them to tell you one story about some event or someone who has had an impact on their career and life. It could be the best boss they ever had, the best team they were ever on, an incredible challenge they overcame, or a huge lesson they learned the hard way. At the same time, images and metaphors are also powerful ways to make points, ways that connect to our right brain. Challenge your clients to think of a metaphor, movie, historical situation, or book that relates to a leadership challenge they are facing. For instance, we can use any number of movies to help motivate someone or a team facing challenges and in need of a turnaround: Rocky is the most overused. You can coach your clients to think of a current movie that applies to their team and how they might use it to communicate their message more powerfully.

Gut. The gut is where we go when we want to hold our ground. It works well when we want to come to terms with the other person, for instance, when negotiating a contract, asserting our needs and wants, and evaluating performance and setting expectations.

Let's suppose we want something and are willing to give something in return. That is a basic negotiation. The format is "If you give me X, I'll give you Y." Notice how this is different from using the head, from using facts and logic. Here we are exchanging things we control. We all control certain things: time, credit, our knowledge, access to us, access to our information, access to resources we control, kind words, and more. For instance, "Joe, if you work for me this weekend, I'll take you and your wife out to dinner next weekend." You can also use negative incentives, if the situation calls for it: "Joe, if you keep coming late to meetings, I'll stop covering for you to your boss." This approach works well when someone is stepping over your legitimate needs and boundaries, such as coming late to meetings.

It works even better if you add a few other statements, for example, what you appreciate or like that the other person is doing, what you don't appreciate or like, and what you expect: "Joe, I really appreciate the knowledge you bring to these meetings, but I don't like that you come late. I want you to start coming on time. If you do, I'll give you more control over the agenda. If you don't, I won't let you lead the product development piece of the project."

This is how we assert appropriately. It works when we match the incentives we offer to the situation. For instance, if Joe has only recently started coming late to meetings, you probably don't want to threaten that you will report him to the CEO of the company. Or, if he reports to you, you probably want to use informal influence first before threatening to put him on probation or firing him. If you have a client who is uncomfortable asserting, you can role play some situations where he has to speak from the gut.

Communicating from the gut also comes into play when we evaluate someone's performance. This is a great way to give informal feedback to each employee or team member instead of waiting for formal reviews: "Mary, I really appreciate the work you are doing on this project, especially the quality of your analyses. If there is one thing I'd like you to change it is that you share your ideas more often in meetings. Going forward, I challenge you to offer up at least one idea every week in our team meetings. If you do, I'll open up opportunities for you to lead a team and work with you on taking more responsibility on the way to the title of Director." Encourage your clients to keep this positive, and only bring up negative incentives if they have been giving this feedback for a long time and an extra push is needed.

Heart. Whereas the head and gut feel directive, the heart is more open. We ask for advice and help. We apologize for past mistakes and offer to make amends. We ask questions and listen. We acknowledge, recognize, celebrate, and thank the other person for his or her talents and contributions. The name says it all: we really are speaking from the heart. This doesn't mean we are wishy-washy. We can still be quite firm, and yet we ask questions and direct the answers we get by listening, reframing, and asking new questions. For instance, "Joe, I'm worried. You keep coming to these meetings late. I feel like I'm doing something that might be causing this, or maybe there is something about these meetings that turns you off. I really want you to come on time because you bring a lot to the team, and I really value your expertise. Please give me your ideas. What will it take to make that happen?"

Now we can listen to Joe. We can be firm and ask questions to involve him while still directing his response. Suppose Joe says, "These meetings are a waste of time and go on too long." Instead of getting defensive, arguing, or pushing back that Joe should come on time anyway, we can involve him again, "I had no idea you felt that way. What ideas do you have to shorten the meetings? How can I make them more valuable for you?" We listen to Joe again. It is up to us to accept his ideas or ask questions to clarify them. Joe might say, "Well, if you could get that agenda out before the meeting and cut Steve off so he doesn't babble, that would be a start." Now we can reply, "I can absolutely get the agenda out. I had no idea Steve was part of the reason you were coming late. Give me some help here. I don't want to embarrass Steve. What are ways I can keep him from dominating meetings without embarrassing him?"

Do you see how this works? We might not be flexible on the outcome we want, but by asking questions, we show we are flexible about how we get there. This only works when we need someone's commitment. If you want them to comply, communicate from the gut. If you want him or her to agree intellectually, communicate from the left brain. As with each of these communication styles, preplanning and role play are effective ways to practice with clients.

Communicating from the heart only works when your clients are willing to be open and honest. If they already know the answer, they are being manipulative if they try to force people to their point of view with questions. In that case, coach the client to just be authentic. Suggest they come out and say what they want and involve people in how best to make that happen.

Spirit and vision. Two communication approaches, spirit and vision, often go well together. We communicate from the spirit and with vision when we want a colleague or our entire team to feel more excited, enthusiastic, engaged, aligned, and energized. This is the realm of the preacher, the politician, and the inspirational speaker. Here, we tap into our shared, deeply held values and our past experiences. We build on the strength of our past relationship. We can also bring up our shared or complementary talents. From there, we paint a picture of a compelling future, a shared vision that others feel part of. We can also insert some of the right-brain methods of communication by using colorful metaphors, telling stories, and referring to heroes from history, literature, and the movies. In other words, communicating with the spirit and with vision incorporates and goes even further than what we covered when we were talking about communicating using the right brain.

Communicating with spirit and with vision is a great way to kick off teams or reengage teams and people that might be down or tired and need that extra push. It is a great way to recruit new hires by getting them excited about what's possible. For instance, "Sue, we both believe in high quality and in going the extra mile. I know we are tired after working nonstop for two months for this very challenging client. Now imagine that together we make a final push to the finish line. We are like the Boston Red Sox coming back from 3 games to 0 to beat the Yankees in the playoffs. A month from now, we are on vacation with our families, glad to be off this project, but also thankful for the huge bonus we received for completing it. At the same time, the firm acknowledges us for our breakthrough work and what it makes possible for others on new projects like this. We are seen as pioneers and thought leaders. What do you see as possible if we make this final push?"

Did you notice how the language changed to use "we"? Did you notice the shared values and history? And did you hear the vision? Here, you include the other person in shaping the vision. You share your vision and then ask him or her to share his or her vision. You are creating a shared, inclusive vision of what's possible. Similarly, one can use spirit and vision to explain to an employee and team about where your organization has been, the values everyone shares, and where the organization is heading. Then your client can ask the employee or members of the team to share their vision about how they fit in and what they see everyone achieving together. Everyone comes together as a team with a shared sense of alignment.

Legs. Finally, we use the Legs when things go wrong while we are communicating. Have you ever been in a meeting where the other person got upset or new facts emerged that threw you off? When this happens, we find a way to excuse ourselves—not to run away but to come back and reconvene when we have had a chance to review our strategy. For instance, "Jill, I see that I said something that got you angry. That was not my intent. Could I suggest we break for lunch and come back to discuss this at 2:00 after we've both had a chance to cool down?"

We might also use this strategy if new information has emerged that causes us to have to rethink our approach and come up with a new plan. If you are coaching a client who is about to go into a high-stakes conversation, ask about situations that might come up in which using the legs is a good strategy. What should your client avoid saying because they know it will frustrate the other person? What might the other person say to your client that could upset them, and how will they react?

Being the message

The most profound coaching on communication focuses on the messages that the client sends with every interaction. Here, you coach clients about how they show up as a leader—or don't—every minute of every day. When we think of communicating powerfully, some people tend to think first about the big, huge motivational speeches, such as in Braveheart, Independence Day, or MacArthur. At the same time, we all know that most communication is nonverbal. Even here, though, we can expand on what communication really means. True, authentic communication means that the leader is the message. People look to the leader for clues about what kinds of things are tolerated and not tolerated, what gets rewarded and what gets ignored or punished, and how things should get done. In this context, the leader is the message. Everything the leader does is the message—far beyond their facial expressions, gestures, and voice tone, although those are important too.

This opens up the opportunity to coach the client if you notice they are not being the message they want to be in any of the following areas:

- Body posture. Do they slouch, stand up straight, walk with confidence, or walk like Eeyore in Winnie the Pooh?

- Facial cues and expressions. Do they show confidence, look angry, look depressed, or look happy and full of possibilities?

- Hand gestures. Do they show nervous twitches, touch their face, hide their hands in their pockets, or gesture with confidence to accentuate their points?

- Dress, hair, accessories, and even hygiene. These all send messages about how your clients think about themselves, their job, and others.

- How they listen. Are they distracted? Do they interrupt? Are they always judging? Are they listening in ways that say they are there to help or in ways that say they already know the answer and are arrogant?

- How they spend their time and with whom. Do they spend more time with their best performers or worst performers? Research shows that the best managers spend the most time with their top performers, which sends a message and also allows your client to work with the people most likely to help them succeed.

- Where they allocate resources and where they don't. We send strong messages based on the projects we approve, those we don't, and those we commit to only halfheartedly. We also send messages through how long we take to make decisions about allocating resources—whether we make rash decisions or are stuck in analysis paralysis, taking too long to decide or being wishy-washy.

- How they react under stress. Does your client get angry, run away, blame, or handle stress with resilience and confidence?

- How they reward success. Is your client stingy? Or are they so generous that people are not hungry and take big rewards for granted, even for insignificant achievements?

- How they react to risk-taking that doesn't work out. Do they punish it, use it as a teachable moment, ignore it, etc.?

- When they give up on an idea or initiative. When do they cave on quality, new ideas, new products, closing a big deal, or ethics? This sends messages to others about when they should quit or cave in.

- When they celebrate success. There are many ways to celebrate success, from a pat on the back to bonuses, awards, and big parties. Different people respond differently. Some like public recognition. Some like private. Some love thatches to acknowledge success. Others prefer cash.

- When they assert themselves and when they don't. People watch your client to see when they take a stand and when they back away.

- How they show they appreciate their employees or members of their team.

- How they show they trust their employees or members of their team.

- How well they know their employees or members of their team.

- How willing they are to go the extra mile.

- How willing they are to be human or vulnerable.

- Their sense of humor.

- Their level of passion.

- When they take personal risks and go out on a limb for an idea, employee, or colleague. Do they support your employees and peers, or do they hold back? Your clients have to be politically savvy, but are they team players?

- How hard do they fight for their ideas while still balancing relationships and results?

- Where they sit in meetings.

- When they do and don't keep their word. Breaking promises, such as coming late for meetings, sends a strong message about character, commitment, and self-perception. So do your clients respond if they have to break a promise. Do they make a flimsy excuse, blame others, or apologize and take full responsibility for their error?

- When they avoid conflict.

- When they push so hard that they come across as inappropriately aggressive.

- What is their orientation to customer service and satisfaction? How often do they talk about the customer? I worked with a CEO who would leave a meeting if the customer wasn't mentioned in the first couple of minutes. He was sending a message about the main priority of his company.

- What is their orientation to quality? Where do they cave on quality? How often do they raise the bar?

- Where do they tolerate low productivity? This sends strong messages about standards.

- What about making financial targets? Your client sets the tone about achieving goals.

The above list is not comprehensive, but it makes the point. Your client sends messages in many ways. As a coach, you can help your clients develop awareness about how they show up as a leader, the messages they send, and how they can be more consistent and intentional.

Influence Others

Leaders get great ideas, sell great ideas, and make great ideas happen. Selling great ideas requires two skills. First, your coaching clients have to know the politics of getting the idea accepted. Once they know whether or not their idea even has a chance and that the battle is worth fighting, they can influence the right people one-on-one to get on their side. Working with clients on their influence is one of the most practical and valuable benefits you can provide as a coach. You can help people become more aware of what it will take to get their ideas to happen and then help them develop the insights and skills to increase the odds of success.

Stakeholder analysis and the politics of getting an idea accepted

Stakeholder analysis is an approach to helping your clients discover if the idea even has a chance to succeed and, if it does, what it will take to get enough people on their side to ensure they can move ahead with it. As a coach, you can help your client get a bird's eye view of the politics of the idea. There are two ways to do this. The first is to create a table that has four columns. An example follows. In the first column, ask your client to list each stakeholder's name.

Next, the client scores each stakeholder based on how much power that person holds specifically in relationship to this decision. A 1 is very little power, and a 3 is lots of power. If the person's power score is a 0, he or she shouldn't be on this grid right now. Remember to coach your client to focus on the person's power in relationship to this decision and not overall in the organization. Power tends to shift based on the issue being discussed.

Third, coach your client to rate the stakeholder's opinion of the idea, from -3 all the way to +3. No 0 is possible here. If your client isn't sure, the client should count the person as a -1. A score of -3 means the stakeholder absolutely hates the idea. The person feels threatened by it and will do whatever it takes to defeat it. A +3 means the opposite: the person totally loves the idea and will go out of his or her way to support it. A +1 means he or she is mildly supportive, while a -1 means he or she is mildly against it. A +2 means he or she supports the idea, and a +2 means he or she really doesn't like the idea.

Often your clients won't know the answer to these questions. That's where you can coach them to get more information either by speaking directly to the stakeholder or by asking others what they think. This approach prevents the person from going full to push on an idea before testing it out a bit to get the general feel of it.

Once the client has filled out the grid, they can multiply out the Power score times the Opinion score and put that in the total column. The score will either be positive or negative, depending on whether the stakeholder has a positive or negative opinion of the idea. If the score is positive, write it down in green. If the score is negative, write it down in red.

Now you and the client have a good color representation of how things stand in relation to the idea. Coach the client to have insights about who supports the idea, who doesn't, how much overall support for the idea exists, whether or not it makes sense to pursue the idea at this time, and what to do next.

Stakeholder Grid

NAME	POWER IN RELATIONSHIP TO DECISION (1, 2, 3)	X OPINION OF IDEA (-3, -2, -1, +1, +2, +3)	= TOTAL

Next, you and your client can map out the grid in organization chart form to get an even better look at the politics of the idea. The process is shown below:

• Draw a traditional organization chart, except:

  * The box size is relative to power in relation to the decision. A person with a Power score of 3 will have a box three times bigger than someone with a Power score of 1.

  * The color of the box is red or green depending on the opinion score.

- Review the organization chart with your client. What does the client notice about the support, or lack thereof, for this idea?

- Help clients assess if they have enough people on their side to win or if this is not a battle worth starting.

- Work with clients to determine a strategy to get enough people on their side to win.

  * Who do they have to influence?

  * Who supports their idea and can influence others?

  * Who do they have to isolate?

- Coach the client to develop a one-on-one influence strategy for each key stakeholder.

Coaching on one-on-one influence conversations

Influence happens one person at a time. In addition to working with your client to map out the politics of an idea, you can also coach people to be more effective in one-on-one influence conversations. Here is a process to do that.

Choose a goal. Many leaders and managers go into high-stakes conversations without a clear goal. You can coach your client to make sure they choose a goal that is specific and measurable. What does your client want the other person to say, think, feel, or do differently, by when? For instance, suppose your client wants Mike to have a better attitude in his job. If your client told this to Mike, he would probably say, "But I do have a good attitude. I show up every day for work and do what I need to do." Now suppose your client tells Mike that he should come to team meetings on time, speak positively about team initiatives, and stop rolling his eyes when people suggest ideas. Now there is something we can measure and even videotape. It is specific and clear, and there is nowhere to hide. Mike either agrees to do it and he does it, or he doesn't.

Assess the situation. After clients choose a goal, coach them to assess the situation. They can develop the best approach to achieve their goal. Coaching questions to ask include the following:

- How is the other person likely to react when you tell them what you want from them?

- What are the other person's motivations in this situation?

- Why will the other person agree with you? In other words, what's in it for them?

- Why will the other person resist?

- What are facts that matter to the other person that would influence them?

- What are things you control (e.g., time, advice, credit, visibility, ability to give more authority) that you can offer the other person if they agree?

- What questions do you have to ask the other person to understand more about their motivation and what can influence them to do what you want?

Plan the approach. After assessing the situation, you can coach the client to develop an approach that will work best in this situation. You might review the different styles of communicating from the previous chapter. For instance, your client can use the left brain to use facts and logic if they want to convince the other person that an idea makes sense. They can use the gut if they have to assert or negotiate and if they care about getting the other person's compliance more than his or her commitment. They can come from the heart if they want to involve the other person and secure their commitment, and if they want to have the other person feel aligned and excited, they can use a combination of spirit and vision and ways of communicating using the right brain. Coach the client on some of the following questions:

- How will you open the conversation?

- How do you expect the other person will react, and how will you respond?

- What objections will the other person raise, and how will you address those?

- How can you avoid having the conversation go in the wrong direction, for instance, by having the other person get angry or too emotional to focus? What will you do if things do go wrong (e.g., find a way to take a break and then get back together)?

- What else do you have to think about to make sure the conversation is successful?

Role play. Role play is almost a must-do when coaching people to have high-stakes or influence conversations. As discussed in the chapter about role play, this is a time when the coach can be quite valuable. A process for role play during influence conversations is as follows:

- Ask the client about how you should play the role of the person being influenced.

- Let clients take a couple of minutes to say everything they really want to say uncensored. Let them have fun and get all the nasty stuff, if any, out of their system.

- Ask the client to practice their opening. Stop and ask what they liked and didn't and what they will do differently next time. Offer your own advice if needed.

- Practice again until the opening is solid.

- Ask the client to practice answering objections. Stop and ask what worked and didn't and what the client will do differently. Offer your own advice as needed. Keep practicing.

- Try different styles: more facts via the left brain, negotiation via the gut, asking questions and listening to secure commitment via the heart, sharing a vision, and appealing to common values and experiences via the spirit.

- Capture lessons learned, and coach the client until they feel they really have it down.

Be sure to follow up after the client has their meeting. There are no guarantees in influence conversations. After the conversation happens, you can coach the client to learn what they can do better and also to decide what to do next in case they don't achieve their influence goal the first time.
Note: Another component of influence is the strength of our network of relationships. A future chapter discusses how to coach your clients to build a strong network.

Manage Time
and Overcome Overwhelm

Time is the most precious asset anyone has. When executives, managers, and up-and-coming talent don't have enough time to do everything they want or need to do, they can start to feel overwhelmed. The coach can help people get back in control and spend their time in the most productive and strategic way. The following process is a simple approach to working with clients who feel overwhelmed or that they are juggling too many priorities and responsibilities.

Clients track their time for a week. Have clients track their time, preferably in 15-minute intervals, for about a week. If needed, the client can track in 30-minute or 60-minute intervals. Create a simple tracking sheet for the client that shows the time intervals and a blank space for the client to track what they do during those intervals.

Evaluate the client's use of time. Start by asking the client what they noticed about how they used their time. What ideas do they already have to be more productive and in control of their time? Then ask the client to highlight areas where:

- They were not focused on something of strategic importance to the organization.
- They could have delegated the activity to someone else.

- The activity didn't need to be done at all.

- The activity was a time waster, for instance, a longer than required lunch.

- The activity didn't need to be done as perfectly as the client did it.

- They could benefit from training to be more efficient, for example, when using a particular technology or process.

- The client tolerated unnecessary interruptions.

- They notice anything else about their use of time.

Work with the client to design an ideal day and week. You can do this in many ways, depending on the client's thinking style. Examples include:

- You and the client take out their online calendar and design the ideal day and week.

- Create a pie graph that shows how major chunks of the client's time are allocated now and how the client wants time to be allocated in the future. A pie graph is helpful when clients also want to reduce the number of hours they spend at the office. The current state could be a large pie graph, and the future state could be a smaller pie graph representing fewer hours worked. Bar graphs can also work, with bands representing different uses of time.

- Redo the activity tracking to represent how the client wants to spend time.

It will be hard to complete this work if clients are not grounded in their most important initiatives and priorities. If you discover that the client is not sure of these, coach them so that they are.

Coach clients to achieve their ideal day and week. Start with general active inquiry to get the client's own ideas. From there, you can more specific questions to help the client get where they want to be:

- What boundaries do you need to set and with whom? Note that this conversation can lead into influence coaching.

- What are your top three priorities? How will you allocate more time to these?

- How can you delegate some of your less strategic activities to others?

- What can you do to reduce the number of meetings you attend?

- What technologies can help you be more productive?

- How can you use a gatekeeper, such as an administrative assistant, to make you less accessible?

- How can you schedule specific activities that you have to do in your calendar so that you are not interrupted except for emergencies?

- How can you schedule in more time for you to recharge so that you can get more done in less time.

- What will you stop doing?

- What will you do less well?

- What limiting beliefs might be making it hard for you to set boundaries or get things done more efficiently?

- How can you set specific times to manage email and texts rather than constantly checking?

- How can you reduce interruptions?

- How can you create more consistent processes that run without you?

- How can you eliminate the need to fight frequent fires by fixing the root cause of the issue?

- How can you prioritize your activities every week and day to be sure you get the most important tasks done first?

The results of this coaching can be profound. I have witnessed executives and managers do this work and get their lives back. They have more time to be with family, enjoy a personal life, focus on what really matters in work and life, and find ways to avoid burning out.

Think Comprehensively About an Issue

A coach can be a great resource to make sure a leader or manager is thinking thoroughly about an issue. A client of mine shared an interesting observation: "I have 15 six-sigma black belts in this organization that can calculate statistics on a variety of quality issues to the thousandth decimal point. However, none of them think practically about how to translate their knowledge to sound, practical solutions." Coaching can help leaders and managers come up with creative, yet practical resolutions to top issues.

First, the coach can work with the client to define the problem accurately. A problem has a current state that isn't acceptable, a clear end state that is acceptable, and a deadline to get there. For instance, "Improve revenues by 25% within six months."

Second, the coach can ask questions that challenge the client to look at the issue from a variety of different perspectives:

- Logical perspectives. Here, a well-trained coach can bring out tried-and-true tools, such as fish bone diagrams and other root cause analyses; six-sigma tools; scenario planning; strategic thinking tools, such as the SWOT analysis or McKinsey 7s framework; systems thinking archetypes; Pareto analyses; and process flow diagrams to help the client think clearly about the issue. Even if coaches don't have training in these tools, they can still challenge clients about their reasoning and logic. They can ask the client about the pros and cons of moving forward with an idea, look at risks, and explore creative alternatives.

- Creative brainstorming. The coach can work with the client to come up with new ideas through creative brainstorming exercises. Some managers rush to solutions and don't consider creative alternatives. The coach can encourage the client to slow down, take a step back, and consider a variety of options.

- Political considerations and stakeholder perspectives. The coach can challenge the client to look at how the issue is perceived by different stakeholders and what that might mean for decisions about moving forward. He can ask how different people involved in the issue perceive the issues, where they have common ground, where they might resist, and how best to accommodate the stakeholders that really matter.

- Shorter- and longer-term views. The coach and client can explore short- and long-term implications of different approaches to resolving the issue.

- Different filters to evaluate alternatives. What if the client looks at the issue financially? Operationally? Technologically? Strategically? Environmentally? Ethically?

- Devil's advocate. The coach can play the role of the devil's advocate and - with the client's permission - try to poke holes in the client's logic.

- Implementation and action planning. How will the issue play out in practical terms? Who is accountable for doing what, and by when? Who should be part of the implementation team? What contingency plans are in place when things go wrong?

Develop Leadership Presence

A common request is "How can I develop leadership presence?" That's a great question because the phrase "leadership presence" could mean almost anything. Take a minute to think about some people you know who need more leadership presence. What would you say are the behaviors, attitudes, and conversations they need to be having? My guess is that if you think of enough people your answers will be all over the map. The most efficacious approach to helping a client develop leadership presence is by using any or all of the tools you already have at your disposal by reading this far in the book:

- Conduct a 360-degree verbal assessment to discover the client's biggest gaps in leadership development.

- Choose a specific behavior that will help the client have more impact. Watch out for general behaviors, such as "have more confidence." Instead, choose a very specific behavior that shows confidence (e.g., walking tall, making eye contact, speaking with more direct phrasing). Create a behavioral coaching process to make the new behavior a habit. When the client succeeds, choose another behavior.

- Use perceptual coaching to help the client overcome any perceptual blocks and improve. Two common limiting beliefs that managers and executives have and that relate to leadership presence are that conflict is bad and they need to be liked.

- Coach them on their communication skills so that they achieve the impact they want to have.

- Help them get better at having influence conversations.

- Coach them to use their time in ways that match how the people perceived as leaders or up-and-coming leaders in the organization use their time.

- Challenge them to think comprehensively about the top issues they have to resolve.

- From there, you can help them build a strong power base of professional relationships, engage their teams, and develop the organization.

Part Five

COACHING SITUATIONS:
STRONG RELATIONSHIPS

Overview

Now that we have covered a few topics related to individual effectiveness, we can move to coaching topics that help leaders and managers strengthen relationships to be even more effective. The topics covered in this section include the following:

- Improve one's power base of professional relationships.
- Engage and mobilize employees.
- Manage up.
- Resolve a conflict.
- Build a great team.

From there, we can explore ways that coaching can move organizational initiatives forward.

Improve One's Power Base of Professional Relationships

Relationships are one of the most important currencies that leaders and managers have. Their power base allows them to make things happen, learn about opportunities before they are posted publicly, and gain access to resources and information that others don't have. Some leaders and managers build their base of professional relationships proactively. Other do this intuitively without thinking about it, and still others have a blind spot when it comes to constantly nurturing and strengthening their professional relationships.

The coach can help in any of these situations by reviewing the client's power base and developing ways to strengthen it. Here are three coaching exercises you can do with your clients, especially those you think can benefit from a review of their power base.

Their organizational power map. Have the client list the most important people in their power base inside the organization. Include employees, colleagues, senior leaders, and any other relevant roles (e.g., outside vendors and advisors). The client should categorize each person in two ways: quality of the relationship and the power the other person has in the organization. Rank the quality of the relationship on a scale of -2 to +2.

- A +2 means that the other person is committed to your client's development and will even take personal risks to support your client's career and success.

- A +1 means that the other person is supportive but won't take personal risks.

- A score of 0 means that the other person is neutral, neither supportive nor unsupportive. It can also mean that they don't know your client well.

- A score of -1 means that the other person is antagonistic toward your client. They generally don't like your client, although they won't go out of that person's way to thwart the individual's career or success.

- A score of -2 is bad news. These are people who are nemeses or foils to your client. For whatever reason, they really want to see the client fail.

Second, rate the power that the other person has in the organization overall. We know that title and power don't always go together. Rate each person on a scale of 1 to 3 in terms of their informal power in the organization regardless of title. A score of 1 represents low power, and a 3 represents high power. Now your client can draw an organization power chart, which is similar to the exercise in the chapter about influence. In this kind of chart, the size of each person's box is proportional to how much power they have. Someone with a power score of 3 has a box three times larger than someone with a power score of 1.

Next, color the border lines of each box according to the quality of the relationship. A +2 gets a double green line. A +1 gets a single green line. A score of 0 gets a yellow line. A -1 gets a single red line. A -2 gets a double red line. This map gives your clients a graphical look at their own power in the organization. After you coach them to have insights about their power, you can work with them on strategies to improve their relationships.

The best way to improve a relationship is usually by improving performance. More subtle strategies will be required at other times, such as asking for advice, developing approaches to help the other person succeed, and getting more visibility by asking to be on initiatives that the other person is leading or involved with in some way. For relationships that are not working, your client might need to think about ways to make amends for past incidents that caused a rift, have a conversation to resolve the conflict, get others to intervene, or find a way to work around the other person. All of these rely on the coach working with the client to understand the other person's motivations, values, personal and professional goals, ways of thinking and making decisions, and communication style. Clients might also have some overall insights about how they show up in the organization, including attitudes and behaviors to change.

Industry and functional power base. If appropriate, you can work with your clients to think about their relationships outside the organization. How can they be more visible in their industry or profession, for instance, by getting involved in professional associations or reaching out to experts in the field?

Power base from the future. The most profound coaching about power base is coaching clients to think about what their power base needs to look like in the future to achieve their overall vision for career success. This kind of coaching is profound because clients will often realize they are or are not showing up as effectively today as they would like. They can identify new behaviors, skills, experiences, and attitudes they need to have to get where they want to be.

The first step in this kind of coaching is for clients to share their vision for their career. What do they want their career to look like in the next five, ten, and even twenty years?

Second, coach clients on who will have to know them and support them for them to achieve their vision. Don't let clients limit their thinking. Challenge them to think about key industry luminaries, opinion leaders, and even legends in the field.

Third, have clients imagine and then tell the story about how they met each of these individuals and developed a strong relationship with them. In other words, the client writes the story as if the relationship had already developed. Sometimes meeting major opinion leaders takes a long time, lots of experience, and a bit of luck. Sometimes, however, we can develop these types of relationships by being active on a nonprofit board, taking on a leadership role in an industry association, or even through a hobby (e.g., religious organization, team tennis league, or a social club). Challenge the client to think creatively.

The final piece of this coaching is to ask clients what they need to change now about how they carry themselves, their attitudes, their behaviors, their skills, and their experiences so that they attract the types of people they want in their future power base. For some clients, this kind of coaching can be an invaluable wake-up call. They realize they haven't been showing up the way they need to in order to attract key people to their professional network. Suddenly, coaching about power base becomes coaching about leadership presence and ways of being.

Engage and Mobilize Employees

Lack of employee engagement is a multibillion dollar problem, with the costs including turnover of top talent, reduced productivity, and absenteeism. According to Gallup's annual employee engagement survey, engagement scores worldwide show lower than desirable levels of engagement and, more disturbing, surprising levels of active disengagement. You can coach managers to be more effective at engaging and mobilizing their teams.

The key to this type of coaching is to get away from blanket generalizations about the manager's overall style or about engaging a monolithic "them." Engagement happens one employee at a time. Therefore, the crucial first step in coaching clients to better engage their team is to list each employee. That opens up the opportunity to develop a strategy for each employee that reports to the client.

For managers that have a huge span of control, with dozens and dozens of direct reports, you can focus first on three types of employees: those that are taking most of the manager's time, those that frustrate the manager the most, and those that are high potentials and need to remain satisfied in their roles. For each employee, the coach and client can discuss the following:

Get to know the employee. What are their talents? What is their communication style? What are their values? How high can they go in the organization, and how high do they want to go? What are their personal goals? By knowing the answers to these questions, your client can have insights about how best to engage the employee. Some employees want to keep moving up, and some don't. Some are happy to work all hours of the day, while others need to be superproductive during normal work hours to get home and take care of their family. Some employees like in-person meetings, while others are more comfortable texting results.

Occasionally, clients will complain that they don't know the answers to these questions. That's a great opportunity for them to sit down with the employee and find out. Another complaint is "I don't have time to get to know my employees." Challenge the client to list any other responsibilities that are more important than engaging employees. Also, the client can do this work over time, for instance, by focusing on a plan for one employee every couple of days.

Set clear expectations with the employee. Managers set the tone in their area of responsibility and get what they tolerate. At the same time, some employees are left wondering how they are doing, waiting for the dreaded annual performance review to find out. Top-performing managers take time to give regular feedback. Sometimes the feedback is about a specific issue, and sometimes it is about overall performance Many managers don't give feedback properly. You can coach your client to be sure stated expectations include the following:

- What they like about the employee's performance.

- What they don't like, if anything.

- What they want the employee to do differently, if anything (sometimes the message is "Keep it up!").

- What they can do for the employee if the employee improves.

- What might happen if the employee doesn't improve (Note: negative incentives should be used sparingly and only when the employee shows a repeated pattern of poor performance).

- Ask "How can I support you in making this change?"

The message can range from "You are doing great and should keep it up" to "I need you to make some major improvements."

Coach clients to customize their leadership style to the employee. Some managers are one-trick ponies when it comes to leading. They use the same approach regardless of the employee's performance and ability to move up in the organization. You can help such managers customize their approach to each employee. Options include the following:

- For poor performers, remove them from the organization.

- For poor performers who have talents that could be useful in a different role, redeploy them.

- For employees who aren't performing well and you can't remove or redeploy, there is no choice but to look over their shoulder and micromanage until you can make a change, especially if they are in a crucial role.

- For employees who have a great attitude and really want to move up but aren't yet ready or aren't performing well, give them some training and oversight to help them develop.

- For employees who used to be performing well but their attitude has slipped (e.g., something is going on at home, or they are frustrated at work for any number of reasons), have a heart-to-heart discussion to find out what happened and what they need to get back on track.

- For employees who are doing fine and are not ready to or interested in making a move, check results, ask how you can support them, and acknowledge them for their good work. Make sure they stay engaged.

- For top performers who are almost ready to move up in the organization or take on more responsibility, become a mentor and guide them to take on more responsibility.

-

Develop ways to recognize and reward employees for their contributions, if appropriate. Many managers are so busy that sometimes they forget that we all appreciate being recognized. Some employees appreciate a pat on the back in private and would be mortified by a public display. Meanwhile, others relish public recognition. Some respond best to a bonus check. Others would be fine with a humorous certificate or trophy. The key is to coach the client to figure out what works best for the specific employee.

Send a complete set of messages to help employees know they are important in the organization. Employees want to know that what they are doing matters and has purpose. They also want to know how they fit into the overall story of where the organization has been and where it is going. A full range of messages includes the following:

- where we have been
- where we are going
- why what we are doing matters, and why what you are doing matters
- our values
- our top strategic initiatives and how your role fits in
- our top performance indicators/metrics as well as yours and how they fit in
- the employee's specific role and how it fits into our vision, mission, and strategy
- what support do you need from me?

Develop the employee. At many organizations, professional development planning is at best an afterthought. It is something managers and employees do to satisfy Human Resources but without much follow-through. In such organizations, you have a great opportunity to coach your client to take a stand for the professional development of each employee. Hold the client accountable for sitting down with each employee, developing a plan for ongoing development with them, and making available the time, experiences, and resources needed for the employee to implement the plan.

Note that the number one way employees develop is through work experience and challenging assignments that help the employee grow. After that come relationships with key people in the organization. Training and development are a distant third. Coach clients to work with each employee to develop a practical plan that will help each member of their team grow.

The final and most important place to coach your clients is on the question "Have you earned the right to lead?" Managers tend to blame their employees first for lack of performance without exploring their own leadership. By conducting a 360-degree verbal assessment of your client's employees, you can find out what your client can do better to earn the right to lead. Typical examples of opportunities to improve are shown below:

- being more positive
- taking a personal interest in each employee
- going first as a leader instead of asking employees to go first
- keeping their word and doing what they say they will do
- respecting employees
- trusting employees to do the job
- avoiding both micromanagement and abdication
- modeling the values and behaviors they expect to see in employees
- setting a tone of excellence

- asking employees for input
- listening
- eliminating nasty behaviors that can destroy motivation (e.g., publicly criticizing, reacting poorly under stress).

One way to have your client identify the behaviors of managers who have earned the right to lead is by asking them about the behaviors of the best manager they ever had. Then ask the client to compare their own leadership style to that of each manager. Coaching on employee engagement can help managers improve productivity, keep and develop top talent, and ultimately have more people on the team to allow them to grow in the organization. Everybody wins with this type of coaching!

Manage Up

Our relationship with our manager is critical to our success, but many executives and leaders do not have as strong a relationship as they would like with their managers. You can coach them to improve that relationship. (If you are coaching somebody who happens to report to you, you can use the framework in this chapter to help them understand how best to improve their relationship with you. At the same time, see the chapter about engaging and mobilizing employees so that the process goes both ways.) The process is simple and applies to improving almost any professional relationship.

First, coach the client to get an in-depth understanding of the manager:

- How do they define success in their role?

- What are their most important priorities and initiatives?

- What are their professional aspirations?

- What are their goals for personal success and fulfillment?

- What is their communication style?

- What are their values?

- What drives and motivates them?

- How do they make decisions (e.g., based on financials, politics, technology, cutting-edge ideas, relationships)?

- What is their tolerance to risk?

- What are their pet peeves, including things to not say or do?

Second, work with clients to assess their current relationship with the manager:

- What does the manager expect your client to achieve?

- What are up to five things they must do well to meet the manager's expectations?

- How would their manager say they are performing?

- How does the manager expect your client to communicate about progress and issues?

- How well would the manager say your client is communicating?

- How well does the manager trust and have confidence in your client?

- How would the manager say your client adapts to their own communication style?

- How committed is your client to helping their manager succeed?

- What past issues, if any, might be causing conflict and need to be cleared up?

- What are the strengths and weaknesses of the relationships?

Third, develop ideas to improve the relationship:

- What is their vision for how the relationship with their manager can be?

- How can they improve their performance, if applicable?

- What does your client need to ask the manager to find out about how they are performing?

- What else does your client need to discuss with their manager, for instance, to clear up past issues or learn more about the manager's expectations?

- How can they help their manager look better in the organization?

- What can they do to help their manager avoid looking bad in the organization?

- What can they do to give their manager more time?

- What can they do to reduce the hassles and headaches their manager experiences?

- How can they help their manager be more successful and achieve their professional and personal goals?

- What judgments do they have to discard about their manager in order to strengthen the relationship?

- What can they do to communicate progress and issues more effectively to their manager?

- What requests do they have to make of their manager but without coming across as entitled?

- What, if anything, can they do to improve their manager's trust and confidence in them?

- How can they build more of a personal relationship with their manager within the limits of what's appropriate?

- How can they do a better job communicating their value to their manager and organization but without being obnoxious about it?

Given your client's answers and insights about the above, develop an action plan that pulls everything together and gets your client into action. If there is a high-stakes conversation your client needs to have, remember the value of role play.

Resolve a Conflict

Executives and managers often struggle with conflicts at work. Sometimes these conflicts are appropriate, based on tensions that naturally exist between different functions and the need for collaboration. However, when conflicts become personal or unproductive and your client is stuck, you can coach them about ways to resolve the conflict.

The first area of inquiry for resolving a conflict is to discover how willing your client is to do what is needed to resolve the conflict. How flexible are they willing to be? What are they willing to do differently or give up? How responsible are they willing to be for the impact they might be having on the other person?

Some people prefer to be self-righteous and stubborn more than they want to resolve the conflict. Your client might want to win at all costs. They might want to see the other person suffer, even if it means hurting results and perhaps their reputation. By starting out with a discussion about how willing the client really is to resolve the conflict, you can get a sense of how successful your coaching will be. Also, by starting here, you can remind the client that they said they were willing to resolve the conflict during times when the other person digs in their heels.

If the client is willing to resolve the conflict, the coaching can follow along these lines:

Understand the other person's position. What is their point of view about the conflict? What motivates them in this situation? What are incentives and pressures that will make this person willing to give ground? What are reasons that might appeal to them? What information does your client need to find out about their position, and who can they ask? What else about the other person's world is important to know?

Understand your client's position. What is the end game? What would it look like if the conflict were resolved? Where are they willing to be flexible? Where are they not willing to compromise? What requests can they make of the other person? Where do they have to make amends for past incidents that caused friction and perhaps resentment? Remember that if the client isn't willing to change anything then the conflict will continue.

Evaluate each party's styles. Sometimes conflicts emerge when two people have very different styles. Ask your client how they might have to adapt to the way the other person things, speaks, or behaves. For instance, suppose that your client focuses on technology and cutting-edge concepts when making decisions, but the other person focuses on financial performance. Challenge the client to consider how the other person is thinking about the situation and how they might adapt to that approach. Similarly, if the other person speaks quickly and gets to the bottom line but your client thinks methodically and needs to talk things out in detail, perhaps your client can learn to adapt more to the other person's communication style.

Find common ground. What do both parties have in common? What are their mutual goals? What are their shared values? Where do they overlap in their vision for what's possible for their organizations? How does this common ground provide openings to resolve the conflict?

With the assessments conducted so far, coach your client to develop the best approach to resolve the conflict. There are many ways to approach someone to resolve the conflict: listen and understand their needs to develop a collaborative solution, make amends for past issues, start a negotiation with give and take, appeal to shared values and a vision for future success, get a trusted third party (perhaps you) to mediate, find someone the other person respects and who can influence the other person to be more flexible, and approach the other person with reasons that will persuade them to move forward in more productive and mutually beneficial ways.

Anticipate objections that the other person will raise and how to handle them.

Consider what might go wrong and how your client can excuse themselves from the meeting before things spiral downhill. If new information emerges or the other person gets angry, the smartest strategy is to take a break, reconsider the approach, and reconvene after everyone has cooled down. Help your clients think about what they will do if the meeting starts to go poorly and they can't think of a way to get it going again. Also, coach your clients about what not to say because the other person will react poorly as well as how they will keep their own cool if the other person says or does something that is inflammatory.

Role play, if appropriate. Once again, role play can serve as an important tool to help your client prepare for a high-stakes meeting with the other party.

The above coaching plan addresses a conflict between your client and another person. What if your client manages a team that has many conflicts? In that case, you can coach your client to look at what they are tolerating. What are they doing, or not doing, to allow these conflicts to happen? How can they get involved to set expectations about the tone of the team? How might they have to change roles and responsibilities? How can they coach team members to resolve their own conflicts?

Build a Great Team

Leading teams causes frustration for many managers and executives. Many reasons account for this dilemma, from lack of a clear goal to unclear roles, personality conflicts, unrealistic timelines and budgets, poor communication, and having gaps in the talent needed to succeed. As a coach, you can help the team leader and members of the team discover what's working well on their teams and what can be better. You can have many different discussions with your clients about their team. In fact, so many books about teams are on the market that you can even buy your favorite book about teams and use it as a guide. Get a copy for your clients, have them read it, and coach them through whatever framework the book uses. In my own coaching, the questions I ask the client include the following:

- What's the specific and measurable goal for the team? Knowing the outcome not only gives the client clarity about how to get there but also serves as a great question to ask when the team gets frustrated. By getting back in touch with the overarching goal and what that makes possible, team members often get back to the work at hand and put conflicts aside.

- What are the roles you need on the team to achieve the goal?

- How will you recruit for the talent you need?

- What are the team values?

- What are the rules of the road about how team members will work together and create a productive environment?

- How do team members know what is expected of them?

- How do team members get feedback about how they are doing and advice about getting better?

- How will team members come together to get to know one another, build chemistry, and come to trust each person on the team?

- What's the plan of action?

- What are the risks, and how will these be prevented and mitigated?

- How can the team get some early wins?

- How often will the team meet to update each other on progress and clear up issues?

- How can the leader ensure there is open, honest communication on the team?

- How will the leader set the tone for a productive team environment?

- How will the leader and team members acknowledge successes and contributions?

- How will the leader and team members make sure that setbacks are discussed openly, in the spirit of learning, so that members can move forward from them and get back on track?

- What motivational strategies work best for each team member, given his or her unique style, aspirations, and drivers?

- How are new people integrated onto the team to make sure they have a smooth transition?

- When people have to leave the team, how is their knowledge captured so that no momentum is lost?

- How can the team come together from time to time to discuss how the team is working and commit to getting even better?

The coach can also play other roles to help the team get better. First, the coach can interview team members from time to time to conduct a 360-degree review of the team. The starting questions are as follows:

- What is the team doing well?
- What is one thing it can do better?
- What other advice do you have to make the team more productive?

From there, the coach can ask team members to assess their individual performance on the team and perhaps also give candid feedback to other members of the team.

A second role for the coach can be as a facilitator. When the team comes together to discuss progress, the coach can step in to review the results of the 360-degree review and also conduct some exercises to improve communication. For instance, the coach can pass out index cards to each team member, one card for each member of the team. Each team member can then give feedback to each member of the team by writing a team member's name on a card and then noting up to three things that the person is doing well and one request for that person to help the team do even better. The cards are passed out to each team member so that each person gets feedback and advice from everybody else. The facilitator can then ask team members to share one new commitment they will make to help the team get better.

Another way the coach can help in a facilitative role is by resolving challenges and conflicts that are coming up on the team. In some cases, my clients ask me to lead entire team retreats over the course of a weekend.

Finally, the coach can also provide training about what makes an effective team. One way to do this is by giving everyone a book about teams to read and having them discuss the contents in the context of their specific team challenges.

Part Six

COACHING SITUATIONS: SUPPORTING ORGANIZATIONAL INITIATIVES

Overview

We have provided examples of coaching to help improve individual performance and to address issues involving relationships and communication with others. Now we can focus on ways that coaching can accelerate and enable major organizational initiatives. This section includes discussions of coaching to:

- plan strategy
- lead change
- develop a pipeline of leaders and plan for succession
- improve employee engagement throughout the organization
- create a high-performance culture
- execute more effectively up, down, and across the organization

In these situations, coaching can have impact as a stand-alone solution. At the same time, savvy leaders know to combine a variety of approaches in any major initiative. Training, facilitation, consulting, incentives, data-driven assessments, new roles and responsibilities, providing sufficient resources, and hiring people with skills not found in the organization can all be components to make sure an organization-wide priority succeeds.

Plan Strategy

Traditionally, leaders hire a consulting firm when the organization struggles developing a strategy to move forward more successfully, but consulting firms have significant disadvantages. They cost a fortune. The consulting process feels invasive, with a bunch of people in dark suits swooping into headquarters even if they have almost no management or industry experience. Once the process is over, the consultants disappear, and the organization has to implement their recommendations, many of which turn out to be a house of cards. Most importantly, it seems disrespectful to the employees of the organization when a company essentially outsources its brain power.

Coaching is a more efficient approach for developing a strategy. A coaching process respects the experience, knowledge, and wisdom of the organization's employees. It relies on leadership to get a conversation going in the organization and make the difficult choices required to set direction. The coach can ask tough questions, keep people on task, serve as a sounding board, speak up when leadership wavers, and assist with implementation support.

In the strategic coaching process I use, the coach guides the client through three phases. While one-on-one and group coaching can help leaders create strategy, this process usually includes a series of strategic retreats, one for each phase. Key executives and managers can come together to discuss the issues, provide input, and get clarity. In between each meeting, the coach and participants conduct research, get input from employees, and collaborate on ideas.

Before the process begins, the client answers questions about the scope of the strategic plan and how it will be completed:

- How far out does the plan go?
- Who is involved as a core part of the team that develops strategy?
- Who provides input, information, and advice?
- When must the strategic plan be completed?
- What is the process to get it reviewed and approved?

How are decisions made? For instance, does a single leader decide based on input, or does a leadership group achieve consensus together? Once these details are clear, the first phase of the coaching seeks clarity about the big-picture strategic questions that every organization needs to answer:

- What is the mission of the organization?
- What is the vision?
- What are the core values?
- Who are our customers, and who should they be?
- What is our best positioning in the market?
- Which products, services, and solutions best serve our customers?
- Who are our competitors, and how do we stay ahead of them?
- What do we do best now, and what should we do best?
- What are our strengths and weaknesses?
- What opportunities and threats do we face?
- How do we build on our strengths and shore up our weaknesses to be ready for the opportunities and protect against threats?

During this phase, it is not essential to dot every "i" and cross every "t." Rather, the conversations uncover potential strategic priorities. By the end of the first phase, the coach and client should have a list of initiatives that could be a focus for the company. Typical examples include improve quality, dominate a particular market, improve innovation, roll out a new product line, test a variety of new products and see which one the market wants, expand into a new market, develop new leadership, and improve process efficiency. Of course, the organization needs to add specifics to these very general ideas.

The second phase of the process reduces the list of potential priorities from many to no more than three. It also results in a tagline or a simple statement that summarizes the strategy so that every employee understands it. Examples include "Beat Google," "Expand internationally," and "Zero Errors!" In this phase, the coach and client develop a process to focus on the few initiatives that will have the most impact on the organization. One way to complete this process is to assign a champion to each potential priority. The champion's task is to create the case for why their priority should be the top strategic priority for the organization. The coach can work with this person to create the case, if needed. The case must include the rationale for the idea, metrics for success, along with what it will take to implement it—from an action plan and risk assessment to the required budget.

During this second phase, which usually culminates in a retreat so that leadership can debate ideas together, each champion makes the case for their assigned priority. Then the participants discuss and rank each priority. A simple voting exercise can take the pulse of the group and discover how much agreement or disagreement exists about direction. Almost every time I have done this kind of exercise a few strategic initiatives tend to receive most of the support. The coach can serve as a facilitator to help the group make progress.

By the end of this phase, the group now has a succinct list of priorities along with a tagline that describes the overall theme or purpose of the strategic direction. Now the process moves to the third phase, which is preparing to implement. One of the biggest complaints leaders have about strategic planning is that the organization takes forever to come up with a strategy and never implements anything. The coach can be especially valuable during this phase of the process.

First, the coach can confirm that the organization has a workable action plan, which includes promises for funding and providing other resources, what the organization will stop doing to free up employees' time, how people will communicate about progress and stay on track, new roles and responsibilities, new compensation and incentives, and new reporting relationship, as appropriate. The coach can serve as a sounding board and devil's advocate to make sure the plan has integrity.

Second, the coach can help resolve issues that come up during implementation. In some cases, the coach can work with leaders to press through unanticipated challenges that come up with almost any new initiative. At the same time, conflicts often arise during implementation, for instance, because a particular executive doesn't want to give up a project or resources that are no longer relevant to the new strategy. In other cases, leaders waver when it comes time to release required resources, setting up employees for failure and frustration. It is tempting for many leaders to avoid these issues and just pile new priorities onto old ones or tell employees to get it done regardless of resources available. The coach can help the organization work through these challenges.

Third, the coach can be a resource to periodically review the strategy and confirm that it still makes sense. Markets change quickly, and organizations need to be always ready to pivot. When new information throws the current strategy into question, the coach can simply ask, "Do you want to do the plan we agreed on, or has new information come up that suggests we should go back to the drawing board and rethink the strategy?" In this way, the coach can make sure that leadership communicates transparently and honestly and keeps the organization informed and aligned.

Throughout the three-phase strategic planning process, the coach can play an important role. The coach can coach leadership through key strategic questions. The coach can help bring together the people with knowledge so that they provide input into the strategy. The coach can support the champions of the potential strategic priorities to make the best case possible for their potential initiatives. The coach can help make sure the overall action plan has organizational support and is realistic. The coach can follow up after the strategic planning process is done to make sure that implementation goes as smoothly as possible and that communication is effective.

Finally, the coach can work with leadership to review the strategic plan and determine when it is time to tweak it or even go back to the drawing board. Shown below is a typical flow for a strategic planning process using the coaching model:

Prework

Coach and client agree on the scope and process for developing the strategic plan, including who is involved.

Phase I: Big-Picture Strategic Questions

- The coach interviews key leaders involved in the process to get their input about the big-picture strategic questions. Prior to the interviews, leaders are expected to get input from their employees and other experts, including advisors, customers, and other constituents.

- The coach synthesizes the interviews to determine where the leadership has consensus and where the leadership has significant disagreements or lack of clarity.

- Coach and client develop an agenda for the first retreat.

- Coach facilitates the first retreat. As the group discusses the big-picture strategic issues, participants are encouraged to identify potential priorities. A scribe tracks these on flip charts.

- At the end of the meeting, the priorities are consolidated where possible to avoid overlap and eliminate purely tactical ideas. A champion is assigned to each remaining priority to develop the best possible business case.

Phase II: Agree on Strategic Priorities

- The coach works with the champions to refine the business case, as appropriate.
- A second retreat is held. During this retreat, each champion makes the case for their assigned strategic priority. The group debates the merits of each priority. A voting exercise takes the pulse of the group. The coach can serve as a facilitator to help the group reach consensus, or the leader can make the final decision about which priorities will be the focus of the strategic plan.
- The coach works with the group to develop an overall message for the organization that succinctly communicates the theme of the strategic plan.
- The champions of the remaining initiatives for the plan are tasked with finalizing an implementation plan for the initiatives. The plan must address how to track progress, required resources and milestones for their release, risk mitigation, how to free up employees to make room for the new initiative, new reward and reporting structures, and any other issues that must be resolved to successfully implement.

Phase III: Implementation

- The coach meets with the champions to help finalize the implementation plan. The coach can ask tough questions to make sure that nothing stands in the way of implementation.

- The leadership team meets to review and agree on the implementation plan. During this time, they commit to releasing resources when required.

- The team creates a communication plan, including a plan about how often they will meet to discuss strategy and clear up issues.

- The coach works with leadership to resolve issues that might come up during the implementation process.

Lead Change

Coaching can be an excellent tool to help leaders and managers in your organization accelerate change. Numerous issues come up to hinder change initiatives. Some can be addressed with the fundamental coaching conversation of active inquiry. Others relate to issues we have already covered, such as influencing others, engaging employees, communicating powerfully, and resolving conflict.

At the same time, you can take your clients through a process to help them have insights about what parts of the change process are working well and which need a plan for improvement. Lines of inquiry include the following:

Assess the organization's readiness for change. Which parts of the organization are ready? Which are not? Who will support the change, and why? Who will resist, and why? Who will have a wait and see attitude?

Anticipate resistance. For those people that will resist the change, what is the strategy to deal with them? What are ways to convince them that the change makes sense? What would be a strategy to isolate, neutralize, or remove them? What are the triggers to put the action plan into place?

Anticipate momentum. For those people that will support the change, how can you leverage them to gain momentum? What roles can they play to lead the change? Who can they influence to get more people on board?

Set clear goals and a vision for change. How will your client know that the change initiative is complete? What metrics define success? What will be possible? What will people be saying and feeling?

Create the case for change. What's the core message to convince people in the organization that the change makes sense? How can supporters spread the case for change without going far astray from the core message?

Go first. Leaders go first during change. How can your clients demonstrate their commitment to the change and model new behaviors and habits? What sacrifices can the leader and others at the top make before asking others to sacrifice?

Set the path for change. What's the plan? Who does what and by when? What are contingencies in case things don't go as planned?

Create teams, if appropriate. What teams can work on specific pieces of the change initiative? Who leads each team? Who participates on each team? How will you make sure these teams are a priority? What will you take off people's plates so they can participate fully?

Provide appropriate support and incentives. What support will people need during the change process? What resources? What training? What political cover? What incentives and rewards? Who will provide this and by when?

Track progress. How will progress be tracked and communicated? Who will compare progress to the plan and make midcourse corrections as needed?

Get quick wins. What is a process to get some initial momentum going by getting some quick wins? How can employees present their ideas for quick wins and have them implemented without bureaucracy?

Develop, sell, and implement ideas. For performance improvement, teams of employees are often the ones who redesign processes and come up with long-term solutions. How can your client make sure there is an easy path for employees to present ideas, have them vetted, and then turn to implementation?

Communicate, communicate, and communicate. What is the plan to communicate progress and other crucial information to the organization? Note that the most effective ways are also the most time consuming—walking the halls, asking how things are going, and having conversations to address people's fears about the process.

Handle setbacks and resistance. During challenging change initiatives, it is not uncommon for the coach and client to spend most of their time on things that are not going well. The coach can play an essential role in making sure the client has a safe, objective person to talk to about what's not working and how to keep moving forward.

Keep setting the tone. Coach the client to set expectations and keep people motivated and on track during the change process. The leader has to continue to go first and set the example.

Celebrate results. How will results be acknowledged and celebrated? How will key contributors be acknowledged for what they are doing to support the change?

As with any significant organizational priority, leading change succeeds when supported by a variety of approaches. Coaching is only one. At the same time, coaching provides a sounding board for leaders to work through complex, often frustrating issues. It is lonely at the top, especially when it comes to change. Coaches give leaders a safe place to vent, test out ideas, and get a source of support.

Develop a Pipeline of Leaders and Plan for Succession

How you coach a business owner, CEO, executive, or manager about succession planning depends on how much of the process is in their control. For some clients, you might focus only on developing potential replacements for their role. For others, you might cover the full range of issues to bake succession planning into the fabric of the organization. Even if your focus with a client is narrow, I suggest that you work with as many leaders as possible in the organization to make sure succession planning is treated as an ongoing, essential process that needs to be baked into the fabric of the organization. Otherwise, the organization will be less likely to grow, attract top talent, and - for for-profit organizations - attain its highest-possible valuation. Also, leaders and managers will not have the leverage they need to focus on strategic issues rather than constantly fighting fires and immediate crises.

Shown below are examples of coaching conversations you can have with your clients about succession planning, depending on the scope of their responsibilities and control. Note that you might have to shift from coach to consultant to facilitator. However, the coaching role is especially powerful because it respects the client's own knowledge and experience.

Use active inquiry to understand what the client means by succession planning. Succession planning means different things to different people, depending on their title and what they want to achieve. Take time to understand what succession planning means for your client. What is a good outcome of a succession plan? At the same time, challenge the client to think about succession planning as a crucial organizational process that should be part of its culture, not just a one-time event to replace a key employee.

Define the future talent needs and roles for the organization. A quarterback throws the ball where the receiver will be, not where he is now. Similarly, organizations need to think about the talent and roles it will need into the future. Coach the client to consider the organization's strategy, future direction, and the types of talent and roles it will need as it evolves.

Plan out the future organization chart(s). A powerful coaching exercise is to have the client map out the current organization chart and then organization charts one, three, and five years into the future. This exercise helps the client see where the organization is, where it needs to go, and what it will take to get there. Based on these charts, work with the client to answer these questions:

- What gaps and risks in key personnel does the client notice in the organization today?

- Who are the top performers who can keep developing and help the organization grow? If the client plays multiple roles, what do clients have to do to delegate more or hire new resources so that they can focus on their most strategic role?

- Looking into the future, what are milestones when the organization will make strategic new hires? Who are the people who need to be prepared to develop and advance into new roles? If your clients are CEOs playing multiple roles, when will they cede those roles to employees so that they can focus on being a true CEO and not a jack-of-all-trades?

Become a talent magnet. Succession planning requires a pipeline of leaders, and that pipeline starts with recruiting. What does the organization need to do so that top talent flocks to it when new jobs open up?

Manage performance to be able to identify top performers. What does the client see as strengths and weaknesses in the organization that affect performance? How are top performers and high-potential employees identified? How are expectations set? How do employees receive ongoing feedback about what they are doing well and can be doing better? How well does management do the job of setting a tone where consistent, high standards are required?

Have a sound professional development planning process to help talent grow. Many organizations have a professional development planning process in name only. Employees fill out an annual form from Human Resources detailing a plan for them to develop professionally, but there is no follow-up. Challenge your clients to develop a development planning process for their organization or for their employees that has teeth, including incentives for both manager and employee when a plan is implemented. What would this kind of process look like at the organization? What role does the manager play? What role does the employee play? What is expected of each party? How will the organization support a strong professional development planning effort? Remember that the top ways people develop in organizations is through challenging work experience and getting to know key people; professional development does not require a massive investment in training programs.

Develop career paths and career plans so that top talent can advance. How does a high-potential employee advance in the organization? For each role that involves leaders and potential leaders, what are potential career paths? If the organization doesn't have clear career paths, what does it have to do to develop them?

Optimize retention strategies to keep top performers. What are compensation packages, incentives, and engagement strategies to keep top performers? How can managers improve their ability to engage top talent so that involuntary turnover of top talent is the lowest in the industry?

Address flight risks. Management should meet every six months to identify high-potential employees that might be thinking of leaving. It can develop strategies to keep key people. Many organizations are blindsided when a top performer decides to leave, and this is inexcusable. Organizations that care about succession planning develop managers who are aware of the attitudes and aspirations of their key people. Coach your client to consider possible flight risks and how to keep good employees engaged and motivated.

Identify roles that need a succession plan. Coach your client to take a look at the current and future organization charts (done previously) and identify the key roles that need a succession plan.

Identify internal people who can fill key roles. In large organizations, succession planning best practice means that each executive has three possible successors, not just one or two. Coach the client to think hard about who can fill key roles and what it will take to get them ready.

Identify roles that will require external hires. Some roles cannot be developed from within, especially newer roles that require specialized technical knowledge. The coach can challenge the client to confirm that an external hire really is required and where to find the talent required.

Develop and test candidates. Finally, after all of the above has been completed, coach and client can develop an action plan to develop and test potential candidates for key roles.

Succession planning is complex and requires a serious commitment, but overlooking this process is much more costly than waiting until the last minute to try to replace someone who leaves a key position. As a coach, you can hold executives and managers accountable for completing a comprehensive succession planning process.

Improve Employee Engagement Throughout the Organization

A previous chapter discussed an approach for coaching managers to be better at engaging their people. This chapter lays out a framework for implementing a comprehensive approach to improving engagement throughout an organization. Coaching plays an important part in this approach but is only one part.

Make the goal of improving engagement a strategic priority. Some organizations have so many programs going on that they treat each one superficially. Improving engagement, as with most other important initiatives, requires focus. If senior leadership doesn't make engagement an area of focus and then get behind it, the organization will not be successful.

Get data with a robust and reliable engagement assessment tool. Measurement is the crux of any change initiative, and engagement is no exception.

Set an overall organizational target for engagement. An overall score gives the organization a target to shoot for and celebrate when they achieve it. The score can be an absolute total or the organization's percentile ranking compared with benchmarks.

Set targets for each manager to improve their specific engagement score. A robust assessment tool breaks out engagement by each manager. This allows the organization to focus on managers that need to make significant improvements. It also makes it possible to give each manager a target to improve engagement and reward managers who succeed.

Look at specific drivers of engagement at the organization and focus there. Many engagement assessments survey the organization to discover what drives engagement at each specific organization. Examples can include how involved employees are in decision-making, whether or not the job provides autonomy, and how much feedback employees receive about their performance.

Train managers on best practices in employee engagement and specifically the most important drivers of engagement. Once data has been collected, the organization can train managers on the key factors in engaging employees and also on how to focus on the most important drivers based on the assessment.

Hold managers accountable for creating and implementing an action plan. Based on their individual engagement scores and what they learned during the training, managers create an action plan and submit it. Achieving this action plan and improving their scores becomes the basis of a portion of their performance review and compensation.

Base a portion of the manager's performance review and compensation on improving engagement scores. If the organization is serious about improving engagement, it has to provide incentives and pressures, which includes putting managers who do a poor job of engaging employees on a probationary period and removing them if they cannot improve their scores.

Put structures in place to give managers more time to engage employees. For instance, one organization realized that managers spent so much time in meetings that they didn't have much time left to meet with and engage employees. They made certain days meeting free and also launched an initiative to eliminate standing meetings that were not productive.

Train internal coaches to work with managers on improving engagement. Coaching reinforces training because it is an ongoing process that looks at real-time events. See the earlier chapter that described a process to coach managers about engaging their employees.

Coach managers who can have the most impact on engagement scores. Few organizations have the resources to coach every manager. The organization can focus on those managers who have the greatest opportunities to improve. Also, group coaching can make the process more efficient.

Senior leadership models the appropriate behaviors. A common frustration among middle managers is that senior leadership doesn't model the behaviors they are expected to demonstrate. For instance, one organization I worked with had respect as one of its core values. One day a senior leader was ruthlessly critical of a middle manager during a major meeting, humiliating him in front of hundreds of colleagues. This leader clearly failed to model the value of respect and never apologized. Employees talk about this incident a year later as an example of senior leadership not modeling the behaviors they want to see and of being hypocrites.

Continue to track engagement scores. Ongoing measurement is required to make sure there is progress and to make midcourse corrections if not.

As you can see, coaching plays an important role in an initiative to improve engagement in an organization. This chapter shows the need for other activities to reinforce coaching and make sure the organization achieves its desired goals. The approach mapped out here applies to almost any other major organizational initiative.

Create a High-Performance Culture

Creating a high-performance culture is a lot like the flow of chocolate down one of those fancy multilayered chocolate fountains you see at weddings. Pure chocolate starts at the top, flows to the next level, and then the next level until it reaches the bottom. In organizations, we want to see the top model the culture, set expectations for the next level to do the same, all the way to the bottom—just like the chocolate fountain. Unfortunately, in many organizations, some layers of the chocolate fountain have something flowing that looks a bit like chocolate but doesn't smell or taste anything like chocolate. The coach's job is to help leadership develop consistent habits, messages, and performance throughout the organization—to make sure the chocolate is pure up, down, and across.

The process of coaching for a high-performance culture is simple. In fact, if you can coach one leader effectively, you can help an organization change its culture. The process involves starting at the top, coaching the top leader or leaders, and then coaching people in each successive layer to spread and reinforce the culture change. Notice that this process is much simpler than the inauthentic and ineffective way that far too many organizations role out culture change. Many organizations make one of three mistakes:

Senior leadership team goes on a luxury retreat somewhere exotic. While swimming and playing golf, they come to an epiphany about how the culture needs to be. Then they come home and expect employees to make the change. Naturally, employees are cynical and resentful because leadership is dumping the hard work on them.

Senior leadership hires a marketing firm to create all sorts of fanfare about the new culture. This turns the culture change into yet another expensive program that never seems to work. Employees see a lot of sizzle but very little substance.

Senior leadership borrows a culture from a successful organization. They adopt the Toyota Way, the Ritz Way, the Disney Way, or whichever company's way seems to be capturing the business world's admiration at the moment. Unsurprisingly, the full culture never seems to translate, and senior leadership looks as if they are attracted to easy answers instead of the hard work of real change.

True culture change requires serious work from those at the top. The top leaders need to take a realistic look at how they are contributing to the current culture, how they are showing up as leaders, what they are tolerating, and changes they need to make to their own attitudes and behaviors. Most senior leaders don't want to bother with this kind of work. It makes them feel vulnerable and is just plain difficult.

If you are lucky enough, however, to be working with leaders who understand the amount of work, introspection, and courage required to really change a culture, you can help them accelerate the change with coaching. Again, the process is simple - if your client is coachable and willing to go through it:

Define the new culture. Coach clients on what they want the new culture to be. Also, what do they like and not like about the current culture?

Get specific by defining performance metrics. Culture is a fuzzy term, often described with descriptive words. Help your client get specific. If the client creates a new culture, how will performance change? What metrics can track success? For instance, when Paul O'Neill took over as CEO of Alcoa, he set a goal to be one of the safest companies in the world.

Similarly, I worked with an executive who wanted his nonprofit organization to be more entrepreneurial, but when we interviewed employees about this change, they had no idea what it meant to be entrepreneurial. The client had to define specific metrics so that everyone understood. In this case, the organization set targets for how much of the organization's revenues should come from grants and fees from the general public as opposed to from government funding.

Get even more specific by defining key habits expected throughout the organization. A culture expresses itself through the habits and behaviors of its people. What new behaviors does your client expect from employees at all levels? Using Paul O'Neill as an example, he set the expectation that when any injury happened at Alcoa, a line of communication would notify each layer of management and then tell him, even if it meant waking him up in the middle of the night. Also, a team would form to make sure that whatever caused the injury never happened again. (You can read more about what O'Neill did in Charles Duhigg's *The Power of Habit*.)

In the case of the nonprofit organization, the leader realized that he needed more of his program managers to start writing grant proposals and also to start charging the general public for the organization's programs rather than offering them for free.

Work first with the top leader or a small group of leaders to model those habits and set expectations. Culture change starts at the top. Too often senior leaders expect the layers below to make changes first. That only creates cynical employees. Coach your clients to model the behaviors they want to see and also start setting new expectations to their direct reports. Behavioral coaching, described in a previous chapter, can be effective here.

Coach the top leader(s) to communicate the culture change to the next level. Once your clients start making changes to their own leadership, their direct reports should start to notice. As soon as the changes have become habits, leaders can communicate their vision for the new culture and performance expectations to their team. This process usually moves ahead through a combination of one-on-one and team meetings. Your client gives specific feedback to each employee during the one-on-one meetings, while team meetings give your client the opportunity to send a consistent message to everyone and get a dialogue going.

Repeat the process of modeling the new behaviors and habits and then moving to the next level and so on. Now you, or a colleague, can coach each member of the client's team to start modeling new habits. Again, behavioral coaching works well here. Once this layer of the organization models the new behaviors, leaders can communicate their expectations to their direct reports, and the process repeats. The chocolate fountain metaphor works well because you and the client work with each level in the organization to ensure consistency and success.

As soon as your clients start making changes to their behavior, culture change can roll out rapidly, but if the client encounters resistance from one or more leaders or managers, you can use active inquiry to develop a plan to help your client handle the challenges.

Why Can't We Execute Effectively?

A common frustration of leaders and managers is that their organization doesn't execute effectively. They can't get things done on time, under budget, with the desired quality. Alternatively, they can't figure out how to solve problems or how to innovate faster than the competition. These complaints present another great opportunity for coaching. As always, the place to begin is with inquiry to better define the problem. Is it an issue with an individual or with a group of individuals who can't seem to execute? Is a team struggling? Is a particular initiative being derailed? Does the entire organization seem to have a culture that keeps things from getting done?

Once the coach knows, they can refine the discussion with the client. For instance, if the issue involves a specific individual who can't seem to execute, the coach can work with them to help them improve. The issue can be one of many:

- limiting perceptions that prevent the person from getting things done, such as a belief that perfection is required

- a behavioral issue, such as procrastination, that causes the person to be late or sloppy with key deliverables

- issues with time management and focusing on the most important priorities

- poor relationships up, down, or across the organization that makes it hard to get things done through other people

- lack of planning or project management skills

- gaps in influence and communication skills

- failure to set high expectations and a strong tone with colleagues and employees
- understanding the conversations that move things forward toward results rather than staying stuck with the status quo

Alternatively, a team might have issues executing. In this case, the coach can work with the team leader and team members to resolve issues. A previous chapter outlined an approach for working with teams, and coaching conversations typically focus on the following:

- setting clear goals
- recruiting the right talents and skills
- having clear roles
- setting clear expectations and holding people accountable for achieving them
- communicating effectively among members and with stakeholders outside the team
- building strong relationships and chemistry so that the team knows each other, cares for each other, and trusts one another
- measuring and tracking key performance indicators
- finding ways to get small victories and gain momentum
- knowing how to have conversations to clear up conflicts and setbacks

Finally, if the entire organization seems to have issues executing, the coach needs to work with senior leadership. Areas of inquiry can include the following:

- how to change the culture with new behaviors, habits, and disciplines
- new roles that might be required

- reducing the number of initiatives to a manageable number
- rewards and incentives that will motivate people
- the ability of management to engage and mobilize teams
- whether or not sufficient resources are made available for success
- whether or not the right people are being recruited
- how people are developed
- which processes need to be redesigned
- how supportive and effective senior leadership is when employees present ideas, when tough decisions need to be made, and when initiatives hit roadblocks

The above issues are only some of the challenges that come up. A coach can help leaders define the problem so that it can be addressed, focus on the root causes of the problem, and find solutions without jumping too quickly to generalizations or superficial conclusions.

Conclusion:

The Crucial, Deceptively Simple Leadership Skill
For Breakaway Performance

The purpose of this book was to demonstrate that coaching is a crucial, deceptively simple leadership skill for breakaway performance. I sincerely hope that you see the power of coaching.

It is crucial because it can help individuals, teams, and the entire organization shift to higher levels of performance. Coaching can turn a manager into a leader who develops leaders and sets up the organization for ongoing success.

It is deceptively simple because it takes practice to let your clients come to their own insights and take accountability for their development and performance. It is easy to slip into other roles that are not coaching and can get in the way of results. True coaching incorporates a bit of martial arts because the best coaches use the client's energy and ideas to help them be successful. They do less and get more.

Finally, coaching - done right - achieves breakaway performance. People in organizations, as well as solo professionals, achieve more when they have support, a sounding board, different perspectives, and the opportunity to think through issues. They also achieve more when they have an environment and process that lets them determine the best course of action for them to develop, achieve ambitious goals, and help the organization progress. Coaching creates that environment and provides that process.

You have now read numerous examples of ways that coaching can bring value. It helps individuals become more effective leaders through coaching on behaviors, perceptions, communication, focus, thinking, and time management. It helps leaders develop stronger relationships to make things happen with the help of others. It also can be a key component in accelerating organizational initiatives, from engaging employees to succession planning and leading change.

If you agree that coaching is powerful, your next step is to practice, practice, and practice some more. Get training to become a better coach. Find colleagues and practice coaching one another. Get a coaching mentor who will observe you in action or listen to recorded coaching conversations that you have. From there, keep encouraging other leaders and managers to master this skill.

It is worth the effort. One coach can help many people get better than they already are. Many coaches can transform an organization.

Addendum One

Seven Habits and a Five-Step Action Plan for a Culture of Success Through Coaching

Creating a culture of success through coaching is relatively simple in theory but hard to implement. This addendum defines what a culture of coaching means and then suggests the high-level action steps required. First, organizations with a culture of coaching have the following habits:

Employees at all levels are open to receiving feedback, input, and advice. In fact, they regularly request it from others. It is not easy to hear tough advice and feedback from others. Most leaders, managers, and employees don't do it well. While the guidelines for receiving feedback are straightforward and the type of skill that is taught in $99 hotel seminars (e.g., thank the other person, treat the advice as a gift, direct it in the way that is most valuable to you, and focus on the issue and not the personal), many people get defensive and are closed to receiving feedback professionally. A culture of coaching starts with employees at all levels being open to advice and feedback. In other words, they are coachable.

Actively strive to get better. Second, a culture of coaching is about mastery. Employees want to keep getting better. They keep raising the bar and demanding the best from themselves and each other. This trait requires an organization with attractive career paths and opportunities for growth and development.

Be willing to stop digging in your heels with stubborn and already known positions and instead conduct a deep, creative inquiry into root causes and innovative solutions. It is easy to have conversations about what's known. It is also easy to stubbornly stick to the same position about an issue so that the issue never gets resolved; for example, watch the political parties in the USA dig in their heels about crucial challenges for the country. In some organizations, employees roll their eyes before a colleague even speaks because they already know what he or she will say. Coaching is about having conversations about what's not known. It is about putting one's position aside and having a dialogue to go beyond rigid thinking and attitudes. Coaching challenges people to leave the past in the past; work together to create new ways of approaching problems; and balance relationships, results, and ego.

Use coaching along with other approaches to develop leaders to grow the organization. A culture of coaching is about developing new capacities in employees. New leaders keep emerging to grow the organization and also allow current leaders to continue to grow and develop in the most strategic ways possible. See the chapter about succession planning for an illustrative approach.

Get important conversations going. The book *Good to Great* by Jim Collins uses the metaphor of a flywheel to talk about one role of a leader. The leader's job is to ask crucial questions about what the organization does best, its values, and its purpose. As the conversations build, so does momentum, the way a flywheel takes a while to turn but eventually becomes a powerful force. A culture of coaching encourages employees to ask deep questions and work together to answer them while always leaving room for new insights and creative approaches.

Create the culture you want to have. A culture of success through coaching is only one aspect of an organization's culture, the same way that coaching is one skill that a manager should possess. Leadership still has to define the complete culture they want for the organization. A previous chapter discusses how to do this work.

Use coaching as a tool to help people get better and continuously improve the organization. Finally, in a culture of success through coaching, people coach each other to ongoing success. This can happen through formal coaching relationships with internal and external coaches, but most of the time it happens through ongoing dialogue with managers, colleagues, and employees. Everyone plays a coaching role.

Action steps to create this kind of culture include the following:

- Train senior leaders and managers to be effective coaches.

- Reward people for modeling coaching behaviors, especially when they solve key issues or develop top talent through coaching.

- Senior leaders need to model the coaching behavior they expect to see.

- Use coaching as a tool to create other aspects of the desired organizational culture.

- Use both internal and external coaches as one of many tools to help people develop.

As with any kind of culture change, the obvious but hard truth is that senior leadership needs to make coaching a priority and a focus. Otherwise, none of the above action steps matter.

Addendum Two

Eight Keys to Creating
a World-Class Internal Coaching Group

As coaching has become an accepted tool to develop talent, many organizations have created internal coaching groups. Internal coaches usually work with leaders just below the senior level, while senior leaders work with external coaches to ensure confidentiality about sensitive initiatives. In our experience at the Center for Executive Coaching, there are eight keys to success when creating an internal coaching group.

Make sure that senior leadership supports the internal coaching group. Senior leadership must view coaching as a crucial function in the organization. Ideally, every senior leader should have a coach to demonstrate how important it is to be coached. If senior leadership doesn't respect coaching or the internal group, neither will others in the organization.

Choose great people to be internal coaches. The U.S. Marine Corps chooses top marines to train new recruits. For a top-tier internal coaching group, insist on only the best people. Some organizations shift mediocre performers to the role of coach. As a result, they lack credibility, and employees don't want coaching from them. Whether you hire coaches from outside the organization or from within, make sure that they are highly respected.

Free up internal coaches to have the time to coach. Too often, internal coaches are given multiple responsibilities, from working on employee assistance to recruiting new candidates. Sometimes this is because it takes the coach time to transition to their new role from their previous job; unless employees make a clean break, they are often stuck straddling two different job descriptions. At other times, the organization doesn't give coaching enough respect and layers on multiple responsibilities. Regardless of the reason, these other obligations often crowd out the coach's ability to coach. If you are going to create an internal coaching group, free up internal coaches to coach full-time.

Don't include progressive discipline or employee assistance under the umbrella of coaching. Coaching is a privilege. It is an approach to make good people better. When organizations combine leadership development with such areas as progressive discipline or any other interventions for struggling employees, they do a disservice to the profession of coaching and what it can accomplish. Separate coaching from other activities. Coaching should focus on helping good people get even better.

Pick a few focused initiatives that are tied to the organization's strategic priorities. Don't set up your coaching group to be a call center to take a call and try to answer questions. Don't dabble in too many initiatives. Coaching should support major organizational initiatives in a focused way. Identify areas where the organization can make key improvements or accelerate progress, especially with strategic priorities. Perhaps certain employees need to develop new competencies to benefit the organization. Perhaps there is a key strategic initiative that has gotten stuck. Or, maybe specific types of people, such as high-potential managers, could make major improvements in their effectiveness that would drive stronger results and competitive positioning. Use coaching to advance these initiatives. That coaching is then tied directly to providing value as defined by the organization.

Use a consistent approach. Some internal coaching groups hire coaches who have been trained in many different ways, which leads to inconsistent results and impact. Choose a coaching methodology and approach, and insist that all coaches use it. At the same time, be flexible enough to test and incorporate new tools, assessments, and methodologies.

Tie coaching to other approaches for developing talent and strengthening the organization. Coaching, training, mentoring, and professional development should all fit together and work toward common goals. Sometimes coaching alone is the best approach. Coaching can often reinforce training programs or other organizational development initiatives. In some cases, a full-court press with multiple approaches is needed to get results.

Measure and track results, and hold the coaching group accountable for having impact in the organization. Coaching is always about getting results, the same as any other function in the organization. Each coaching relationship should start with a clear intent and outcome. From there, track results of every relationship. Tracking results means more than asking clients about whether or not they were happy with the coaching. Specific, measurable improvements should show up in the organization from each coaching engagement. Results can range from tangible financial improvements to how confident and competent the client feels about using a new skill. Regardless, coaching should be as accountable as any other function in an organization.

About the Author

Andrew Neitlich is the founder and director of the Center for Executive Coaching (http://centerforexecutivecoaching.com), a leading coach training organization. The Center for Executive Coaching has been training coaches for a decade and is an Approved Coach Training Program (ACTP) with the International Coach Federation and also approved to provide training hours for the Board Certified Coach (BCC) certification. Members include professionals who have held leadership roles in many organizations, including FedEx, Aflac, Microsoft, Cisco Systems, Ascension Healthcare, Kaiser Permanente, the United States Air Force, Florida Institute of Technology, University of Minnesota, the United States Department of Defense, Macy's, the NBA, and Deloitte Consulting. Andrew also developed the Coach Master Toolkit, a library of practical, results-driven coaching methodologies. He has trained over 1,000 coaches around the world.

Andrew received his MBA from Harvard Business School in 1991. In addition to leading the Center for Executive Coaching and running a full leadership coaching practice, he is the author of the following books: Elegant Leadership: Simple Strategies, Remarkable Results; The Way to Coach Executives; Guerrilla Marketing for Coaches; and Guerrilla Marketing for a Bulletproof Career (both with Guerrilla Marketing founder Jay Conrad Levinson). He lives in Sarasota, Florida, with his family and plays lots of tennis.

For Additional Resources about Coaching, Coach Training, and Coaching for Your Current and Future Leaders.

The Center for Executive Coaching is available to train you and your team in the best practices of executive and leadership coaching. We have a number of solutions, from full training and certification to the use of our Coach Master Toolkit, along with online training programs for managers to learn coaching skills. We can also provide you with top-tier executives and leadership coaches to help your leaders and high-potential managers get even better.

For more information, visit us at http://centerforexecutivecoaching.com
or contact Andrew Neitlich directly
at andrewneitlich@centerforexecutivecoaching.com.

CPSIA information can be obtained at www.ICGtesting.com
Printed in the USA
BVOW08*0141020816

457637BV00002B/4/P